EMPIRE ᴇ ᴊᴅᴇᴅ

A Modern Man's Path Back to His Tribe

By Jeff Putnam

For my wife and children who make my life better every day.

FORWARD

What is an empire?

An empire is ultimately an extensive group of states or countries governed by a singular supreme authority such as an emperor or empress. It can also be defined as a large commercial organization that is either owned or majoritively controlled by one person or group.

Although each empire throughout history has been somewhat different as far as how they were built, there are seven major characteristics that every empire since the dawn of man has possessed, the first of which is a strong government. Due to their sheer size, empires required a strong governing body that was centralized meaning that it allowed for little to no discretionary variation in the rules and regulations that it had decided on by anyone but the government itself.

Empires are bureaucracies in which they appoint non-elected officials to manage their citizens, resources and territories, leaving the people very little choice in how they live their lives. There is a strong sense of militarism where the empire has the right to exercise at its own discretion, the ability to enforce and control its territories and everything within them. There are global trade networks that use commerce as a means to connect with other empires and share resources.

They are standardized in their laws and currency in order to effectively maintain an efficient level of control over its entirety rather than allowing any single part or state to determine its own which would only bring confusion and a lack of cohesion between its parts. They all established infrastructure and public works such as roads, and water systems that were all paid for by the citizens under the control of the empire through a tax system.

And lastly, every empire in the history of man was made possible by the execution of a unification strategy. Empires are largely diverse populations that are made up of various cultures, religions, and backgrounds that were once independent of one another that had either been conquered or had chosen to become a part of the empire through some treaty or deal to ensure they survived eradication.

In order to bring these vastly different people together, an empire had to devise and put strategies in place that were meant to bring people together and make them each feel that they were a part of the empire. The idea was that the conquered or acquired people would be able to retain certain aspects of their former identities while simultaneously adopting many of the new ways of their empire to become a working part of the system that could interact evenly with all other parts of the empire.

Today, there are no official empires left on earth. Although should some countries decide to embrace their empirical destinies at some time in the future, that could change. Until that day comes however, the ghosts of empires past still continue to stalk the earth from within the shadows. Even the United States is haunted by the spirits of ancient empires that have long fallen.

Nearly everything about the U.S. was derived and modeled from the ancient Roman Empire from its form of government, all the way down to its architecture. Even the birth of the U.S. shares similarities with the birth of the Roman Empire. Romulus and Remus both once belonged to another kingdom when they set out with other like-minded villagers to create their own city within the same kingdom much like the citizens of the British Empire left to start a colony across the Atlantic that was controlled by the British so you could say that the United States is one of those few countries with an empirical destiny as well as origin.

While America doesn't, at least overtly, seek to control other territories and people abroad, it is more of an indirect empire, but an empire nonetheless in that it maintains all seven of the major characteristics of one. Furthermore in its current state the United States of America has also come to embody the second definition of an empire in which it has become *commercialized* and wrought with consumeristic traits of a corporation and being run by a particular group of people with a particular set of interests and control.

This commercialization of America is even more noticeable when you look at the current political state of affairs and how there seems to be a fervent push towards the adoption of a more unified and global identity that is very similar to that of one corporation merging with another. This will no doubt lead to many changes in the current standardization of laws and ethics as compromises and adjustments are made in the spirit of unification with the rest of the world under an even more centralized state of control and governance.

A new global empire.

Much like the fall of the Roman Empire was brought about by the mass influx of corruption, greed, cultural division, personal ambitions and frankly self-serving nature of the bureaucrats that had been appointed to govern, the U.S. has begun to follow the same path toward its empirical destiny.

As it is, too many cultural and morally ethical differences exist and even with the compromises that have been put into place to unify them, have started to divide themselves from the empire as they become more and more dissatisfied with the way the empire regards them. It isn't a stretch to assume that the further expansion through globalization will only act to further drive a wedge between the empire and those that are already pulling at its seams.

Quite frankly, there just aren't enough compromises that can be made to appease them. As more cultural compromises are made, people are being forced to abandon more and more of who they once were and contrary to the wishes of the empire, it isn't going as expected. This ideal of total unity under a singular banner of an empire ruled over by a governing body of elitists who are altruistic in nature spells a recipe for rebellion and collapse.

Should the citizens of the empire make the impossible choice to abandon their own identities and everything that makes them who they are, they will disappear into an oblivion and be ruled over by an empire built of nothing. This *empire of nothing* as it is referred to by author Jack Donovan in his books, The Way of Men, and Becoming a Barbarian, and A More Complete Beast which were the inspiration for this work, offers no solace to a man whose very nature compels him to search ever forward to discover who he truly is.

Instead, men and their ancestors upon whose backs the great empires were built are cast aside, told that they are no longer necessary and that the very things that make them who they are have no place within the walls of the empire. Men are now branded as toxic and their nature must be eradicated in the name of progress. But man was bred for war and to quote Dylan Thomas, will rage against the dying of the light.

For years I myself have struggled to find some connection between the world that I have been shown through the lens of modernity and the world that I feel with every part of my being. A war of attrition has been waged for the souls of the men of the empire and the invasion has not gone unnoticed. Sadly, only a few have been willing to acknowledge the fight much less fight it.

The truth is that this war cannot be fought from within. In order to become the man he is destined to be, one must reject the empire and those that choose to remain its citizens. He must realize that he is not one of them and they are not his people. He owes them no allegiance despite what he has been programmed to think.

Like what I imagine to be the struggle of every man as some point or another, I have struggled to find where I fit in this world. Like many men I have often dreamed of being born to another era in some far and distant land where I imagined that life would be much simpler than it is today. Now obviously this is delusional. While the daily challenges that we face may be vastly different, the world is no more complicated today than it was 1000 years ago. I'm even willing to bet that the men born in the dark ages had the exact same thoughts of being born late into a world that they didn't feel they belonged to.

The truth is that men do not belong to the world, but the world to them. The world of their own making is theirs and the empire has left men with no alternatives but to rebel. This *react-ance* is present in all men. Man is hardwired to resist the theft of his freedom and sovereignty.

He feels it deep in his balls. He is not meant to be a slave. He is meant to rise, defend his perimeter, and to conquer.

He is meant for the tribe.

CHAPTER ONE
COURAGE

*Out of the night that covers me, Black as the pit from pole to pole,
I thank whatever gods may be for my unconquerable soul.*

*In the fell clutch of circumstance I have not winced nor cried aloud.
Under the bludgeonings of chance, my head is bloody, but unbowed.*

*Beyond this place of wrath and tears Looms but
the Horror of the shade, And yet the menace of the
years finds and shall find me unafraid.*

*It matters not how strait the gate, how charged with punishments
the scroll. I am the master of my fate. I am the captain of my soul.*
Invictus
-William Ernst Henley

Described as a rallying cry to those who find themselves thrashing about in the darkness of hard and trying times, Invictus is one of the world's most well-known poems. Nelson Mandela said that he recited it numerous times during his imprisonment. He did this to remind himself that it was his courage that would see him through, no matter the end.

When we hear the word courage today, we imagine a romanticized idea of what courage looks like. For me, it's always the same thing. It is the berserker standing alone in the middle of Stamford Bridge while facing an army of 15,000 Saxons so that his clan could maneuver for a strategic retreat.

As the historical account tells it, he held the bridge alone, striking down 40 men with his Dane Ax. He allowed no one to pass before the English sent men with pikes and spears beneath the bridge to stab at him from underneath while he was engaged with other fighters. While there is little to no chance of an opportunity to engage in such an incredible act of courage today, courage is nonetheless imperative to a man's being. I don't foresee myself marching into battle, skeggox in hand, and ready to meet my enemies any time soon. Still, each day allows me to do battle with a relentless and omnipresent foe.

Myself.

Molded by the ease and convenience of the modern world, man is drawn on the surface, to the path of least resistance, yet to take it leaves him feeling restless and unfulfilled. Deep inside him stirs a beast, a warrior, a man in his purest form just waiting to be unleashed. It takes courage to march into battle with oneself and live a life where every decision made is intentional and has a purpose. The man within is not at all suited for a life of ease.

He lusts for new lands and people to conquer. Things that are generally frowned upon in a civilized society. Yet to deny this indulgence is to deny who we truly are as men. We were not bred or evolved for comfort. We were bred for war, and we must show the courage to wage it. Even if the enemy is staring at us in the mirror.

So how does a man in the modern world show true courage in the world he lives in? The empire is a thief in that it has robbed men of the opportunity to become great. You don't really have to be all that brave to go to work, the grocery store, or just outside to throw some steaks on the grill. As of the time of this writing, there are no bandits nor Mongol hordes roaming the streets trying to kill you and ransack your village. There aren't any warring clans seeking to use you as a sacrifice for their gods or take your resources and women.

So again, I ask, how is a man supposed to show courage, *real courage* today? To answer this question, we have to answer a few others. What is the definition of courage? Put plainly, it is merely the willingness to act even in the face of fear and full acknowledgment of the potential consequences.

But what is there to be afraid of anymore? You can go and do whatever you want, wherever you want today, with little to no risk to your own safety in most, if not all, first-world societies. The concept of courage itself has become watered down. T.V. and internet celebrities are often referred to as courageous when they decide to "come out" as gay or transsexual. If they have an opinion that goes against the status quo, they are seen as brave. In reality, unless you're living in a third-world country where saying such things will get you killed, the courage required to do these things is over-exaggerated and overvalued.

Suppose acting courageously in civil society requires the presence of fear. In that case, for fear to be present, there must also be implied risk. The greater the risk, the greater the amount of courage required. The less risk, the less courage is needed, and ultimately the value of that courage is greatly diminished. The risk associated with coming out or speaking out today is little more than some hurt feelings or perhaps losing a job. While it can be devastating to many, it still beats taking an ax to the face at the hand of a fearsome enemy. This isn't necessarily all that bad. Living in a society where the risk of being attacked by a random enemy on a daily basis is a good thing, but the caveat is that we end up having little to nothing to fear and, by that measure, no real opportunity to be courageous.

In order to find opportunities for traditional courage outside of joining the military, law enforcement, or a local fire department, we need to try to find the equitable risk of our own time.

The old phrase, *you are your own worst enemy* still holds true even today. Whether through self-doubt, self-sabotage, complacency, apathy, or even nihilistic philosophies that seems to be growing more and more prevalent as our modern world slips into a more secular collective.

You can often see this displayed through social media arguments between the faithful and the faithless. Having faith in something requires an act of inner and more personal courage than that of the kind of courage you would see on the battlefield. Risk is present in the manner that if you're wrong, you're going to someplace that you're not going to like very much in the event of your inevitable death.

Having faith in oneself also requires courage that is sometimes considered irrational or unjustified courage. Believing that you can achieve a goal with no past track record of being an achiever is unjustified. Does a soldier who has gone to war multiple times have courage? Of course, he does, and it is by all means justified. But the new soldier, the one who has never seen a battle yet willfully walks into the flames of war, also has courage, but this is an irrational and unjustified measure of it.

It's easy to put on a brave face and act courageously when doing something you've done before. Even if the risk is still there, the experience gained from having gone through something fearsome before reduces the amount of courage required.

The Havamal, which roughly translates to *Words of The High One,* is a poem of collective Norse wisdom taught by Odin. It is thought to have been written between 858 and 1250 AD. In the 16th stanza of the Havamal it says, *"A coward thinks he will ever live, if warfare he avoids; but old age will give him no peace, though spears may spare him."* This appears to be talking about the consequences of avoiding battle and being left with regrets that will follow you throughout your final years. As I mentioned before, these opportunities for battle in today's world are few and far between.

This brings us back to being our own worst enemy. We still have the opportunity to go into a battle each and every day, even if it's not a battle in the traditional sense of the word. Each day we are faced with choices that will take us down one path or another, and as humans, it is within our nature to always choose the course with the least amount of obstacles. The need for comfort and efficiency often overrides our biological need to conquer new lands and achieve new heights or status. In order to combat these tendencies, a man must be intentional with his endeavors and not fall into the trap of promised comfort and ease.

The act of intentionally seeking out hardships or the path of most resistance requires courage and a certain amount of self-belief, just like the soldier who willingly goes into battle for the first time. This is not to downplay the soldier by any means. This is merely an analogy meant to convey the need for courage when facing the unknown and its unforeseeable risks. To challenge oneself is the ultimate form of sacrifice that we can achieve in today's world. In doing so, we risk revealing things about ourselves that could shatter our previously held identities and make us finally face who we truly are.

A man will naturally hold himself in high regard amongst his peers until his mettle is tested and he is proven otherwise. Asking, *"Am I enough?"* leads men to measure themselves against other men, and the risk of discovering that we do not can shatter our ego and confidence. Taking on challenges that will test our merit is not something that comes easily, but it is required if a man wishes to discover who he truly is.

A common theme that often comes up is that we need to return to the type of lives our ancestors lived hundreds of years ago. Well, I don't know about you, but I'm a pretty big fan of indoor plumbing and clean drinking water. Yes, it is true that our predecessors were stronger and far more capable than we are today at survival. But that is because it was necessary for them. If they had failed, you wouldn't be sitting here reading this book.

No, I don't think that we should go back or regress to the way of life as it was lived hundreds or even thousands of years ago. Our ancestors did what was needed out of both necessity and the desire to make their children's tomorrow better and easier, much like we continue to do today. The fact remains, we evolved to live a much harder life than the one we have today.

However, the unintended consequences of these wholly natural and noble endeavors have brought us to where we are today. This is a world where we, as men, are afforded luxury over challenge at every turn. This is what our ancestors wanted for us. To live as they saw the kings and jarls of their time did. Even though it has made us softer and more pliable as industrialization and technological innovation continue to progress.

Slow Wi-Fi and long waits in Monday morning traffic aren't hardships. They are minor inconveniences. Yet, we still tend to behave as if they were some major difficulty. Our bodies and minds are built for a life much more difficult. We tend to *come alive* when we are faced with challenges that test our mettle and strength. We seek out minor conflicts on social media and with our peers. We gather around the tv to watch ritualized war in the form of sports and other activities that require courage and grit because deep inside, that need for courage is still there.

If we are to live courageously, then we have no other choice than to embark on endeavors that make us uncomfortable in the world that we have. We can't and shouldn't go back to a more primitive time, and to do so would dishonor those that came before us. Instead, we should be doing battle with the man in the mirror and with our weakness and comfort. We must be willing to face the fears of today. We must resist the pull of the current and live intentional lives.

Living with intent can be uncomfortable to people who have spent their entire lives just *going with the flow.* It requires courage to act decisively when faced with choices that could impact our lives. It takes courage to walk into the gym for the very first time and stand among bodybuilders and powerlifters. As many others can also relate, the first day in the gym can be intimidating, especially if you have no idea what you're doing. While the risk may not be physical, the fear of being laughed at by stronger men is real. It can sometimes be debilitating enough to ensure that day two in the gym never comes.

Most if not all of the members are significantly bigger and stronger than you, and you cannot help but feel as if every bit of you is being scrutinized, and to some degree, you absolutely are. Look on any social media site, and you can find scores of videos and viral threads of some poor individual being laughed at and made fun of as he makes an absolute fool of himself on some machine that he has no idea how to use.

You can find complete threads and forums filled with experienced weightlifters having a go at an individual who just started, mocking his lack of strength and proper form. Because these are so easy to find, it isn't difficult to mistake this for being the norm when in fact, these guys are really just a bunch of assholes and only make up a small minority of the lifting community.

Many experienced lifters will, in fact, offer help and guidance to the newest and most inexperienced members. This is because the lifting community really is a tribe to a certain degree. One extreme example is the more recent phenomenon and rise of group gym clubs such as CrossFit. Here you will see the members rallying behind and cheering on each individual as they all participate as a collective, rather than the individuals you find in most traditional gyms. But even the gyms that don't offer group workouts are still a community, although it isn't as blatantly obvious to beginners.

There is an unspoken mutual respect that fellow lifters afford each other as they see them more and more often, and remaining consistent with their efforts. They know the level of self-discipline and courage that is required of someone who joins a gym looking to become bigger, faster, and stronger. They know all about the initial fear and uncertainty that was felt because they had also felt it when they first began.

Once he realizes this, the fear and discomfort all but disappears from the mind of the beginner, and he is slowly absorbed, seemingly passively into the tribe, and he is now *one of them*. But to get to this point, it still required courage and the willingness to commit even with the risk of ending up a laughingstock on social media.

It takes courage to marry and raise a family that we must support and lead through our own merits and actions. All you have to do is look at the statistics of divorce rates and fatherless homes or the number of men who lost nearly everything in their divorce who shout from the rooftop to anyone who will listen, their warnings against marriage.

It's no secret that the courts are more likely to award a soon-to-be-divorced woman the better end of the deal. More times than not, they end up with full custody of the children and financial support. All while the burden of compliance falls on the shoulders of the man, or else he faces the full loss of his freedom through incarceration.

These kinds of risks have led to the recent birth of subcultures such as *The Red Pill Movement* or MGTOW, which is an abbreviation for *Men Going Their Own Way.* While these subcultures exist to serve a purpose and neither of them is inherently bad, at least in the beginning, they failed to offer their members a pathway to evolution and eventually became an echo chamber for scorned men railing against the evils of women and their betrayal.

The Red Pill or TRP was coined from the movie The Matrix, where the main protagonist Neo was offered a choice between a red or a blue pill by Morpheus. The red pill would allow him to go further down the rabbit hole and discover the truth about the world he only thought he knew. Should he choose the blue pill, he would be granted the opportunity to remain blissfully unaware of these truths and return to his former existence.

The Red Pill Movement offered to show men the reality of intersexual dynamics and teach them how to successfully navigate the biological, psychological, and evolutionary differences between men and women in the world as it is today. The MGTOW subculture was to be a sort of psychological haven for men who had been burned by the fairer sex either through the process of divorce, a failed relationship, or by simply being ignored completely and rejected.

The problem was again, the lack of an evolutionary path, and each group eventually became a beacon that only attracted *victims*. Rather than focusing on the betterment or empowerment of men, they justified their fears of being hurt and rejected. Much like a wounded animal caught in a trap or a dog that's been beaten by a previous owner, the members of these communities began lashing out at anyone without a penis in fear of experiencing more pain.

While these fears are valid, they are not and should not be considered the endpoint for men who have gone through them. Nor should they be used to discourage any man from finding a wife and starting a family. Just like courage must be an intentional act, so should the process of finding a suitable wife, mitigating the risk of divorce through properly vetting a woman's eligibility for wifehood, and starting a family that men have the responsibility to lead.

It is a misconception that the family man took the easy path, whereas the single *playboy* is on a much more difficult one as he tries to navigate the world for the purpose of unending sexual conquests. It's true that the latter is essentially always *on the hunt,* but he ultimately remains safe from risks by being emotionally detached from anyone or any possibility of an actual committed relationship.

The man who chooses to be a husband and father shows courage because he knows the risks are great but not nearly as great as the reward. He knows that leading his wife and children is a task not suited for the weak and faint of heart, yet he rises to the challenge because it is who he is meant to be as a man.

When it comes to fatherhood, I can't think of anything more terrifying or fulfilling. The world that we have now isn't one that is ideal for raising children. With the courts being in favor of women, becoming a father comes with the risk of losing one's children in a bitter custody battle. It comes with a deep responsibility to form young boys into men and young girls into women. And not just any men and women, but good men and women who are good at being men and women.

Being charged as the leader and head of his family rests squarely on the shoulders of a father to lead by example, teach, and, when necessary, to discipline and provide guidance to his children. This is no easy task as he must fight to remain the most prominent influence on his children. This hyper connected world of information and connectivity through social media will always be a battle where the odds are stacked against him.

Being a good father, a good husband, and a good man is nothing without being good at being those things as well. In his book, The Way of Men, Jack Donovan speaks frequently about the differences between being a good man and being good at being a man.

"There is a difference between being a good man and being good

at being a man. Being a good man has to do with ideas about morality, ethics, religion, and behaving productively within a given civilizational structure. Being good at being a man is about showing other men that you are the kind of guy they'd want on their team if shit hits the fan."

You can obviously be a good man without being good at being a man, just like you can be good at being a man without being a good man. Being a good man simply means that you have a penis, and you abide by the code of morals and ethics laid by society. Being good at being a man requires much more. It takes relentless effort and courage to be both and in order to be a complete man, it is required.

You cannot, however, be a good father or husband without being good at being them. If all you do is show up and make sure that their basic needs are met and ensure that no one dies or gets hurt in the process, you're only covering the bare minimum, and that isn't good enough. Being good at being a husband and father requires you to be both a good man and be good at being a man.

In order to be good at being a man, you must face yourself and all of your shortcomings and fix them while leading your wife and children to do the same. This is no easy feat and requires great courage, especially when you consider all of the risks that come with getting married and having children at all.

It takes courage to be good at being a man in a world that seems to have all but decided that men are an unnecessary inconvenience. Today, anything you say or do will be scrutinized and picked apart by nearly everyone to ensure that you don't possess *wrong thinking* or lack political correctness. The world has shifted from a time where meritocracy takes precedence over inclusiveness. In fact, any form of exclusivity is now considered to be one -*ism* or another or is labeled as phobic by the elites whose only goal is to secure as many votes as possible.

These people that sit in government office buildings writing new legislation and policies based on inclusiveness and fairness all have one thing in common. They are the good citizens of the empire and aspire to force everyone else to be the same. After all, they know what's best for you better than you do. The sad irony of this is that for all their pandering and theatrics about equality and vying for a society that is fair and equal to everyone and everything for the sake of public interest, they still act as if they know that their way is the right way and anyone who doesn't see things the way that they do is not to be considered *one of them*.

This isn't just a display of hypocrisy but also of arrogance and exclusivity. They know that they aren't truly capable of giving a shit about everyone everywhere at the exact same time, yet they still put on their little song and dance for the people who have resigned themselves to being mere subjects rather than citizens. The convenient interchangeability of labels makes the lie oh so believable to those that kneel at the teat of the empire hoping for a drink.

The leaders of the empire stand atop their soapboxes preaching unity, yet their words are laced with the ever-unifying idea of *us vs. them.* The only real way to unify a group of people is to rally them around a common cause, value, or against a common enemy that threatens their way of life. Without a *them,* there can be no *us,* so they speak to the masses in circles with double talk and self-fulfilling prophecies to ensure that the lie proves itself to be true. They curry the favor of the mob while still placing themselves in their own position of *better than you.*

The common enemy of the empire is anyone who is not willfully drinking the Kool-Aid, and they are still plenty. Hell, even the Jim Jones cult had members who were backing out in the final hour and were held down and forced to drink by the true believers on November 18th, 1978. As far as the empire is concerned, if you aren't a true unquestioning believer, you must become one by force or else. This is nothing more than a modern reversion to a *convert or kill* based religion.

The idea of convert or kill has long been a tenet of Abrahamic religions. Islam and Christianity alike both have deep histories of killing anyone who wasn't one of their tribe through their efforts to expand and conquer new peoples to bring them into the fold. The idea was that the bigger the tribe, the stronger it would be, which makes sense, at least at first.

Today we have a more civil and mostly nonviolent equivalent of convert or kill. Anyone that doesn't toe-the-line with the empire's virtues or speaks their own mind is now attacked by the mob in what has become known as *cancel culture*. Any man or woman that comes under fire by the mob is publicly threatened with the loss of their livelihood or status unless they kneel, submit, and bow to the mob's demands for a public apology and the retraction of whatever incorrect opinion they had.

The empire is a land of unity and equality and tolerance, so long as you think, speak, and act in goose step with everyone else. Those who show the courage to refuse the mob's demand are vilified and ostracized from the collective and cast out from the empire while being labeled as *one of them*. The independent and free-thinking man who chooses to care for his own people and disregards everyone else has become today's barbarian.

In ancient times, the word *barbarian* had a different meaning than what we associate it with today. We hear the word and instantly think of huge guys with knotted muscles, beards, and wearing animal furs. But in ancient times, the barbarians were simply members of any community or tribe not belonging to one of the great and peaceful civilizations (Greek, Roman, Christian), meaning that they didn't recognize their culture or their way of life. They lived both inside and outside of their own nations, walking within the lines of geographic proximity to their more "progressive" neighbors, while rejecting their corruption and false virtues, which created a continental divide between the two.

The barbarian cultures were primarily based on strength, utility, honor, and the passing down of stories within a tribe. This was unwelcome within the walls of the empire where status was granted not by honor gained in battle or by contribution to the tribe, but by the weight of a coin purse and forked tongues lashed about in darkness, making shady deals that were hidden from the peasants. Like today, status was held by those that felt like they knew what was best for the people and that it was their highest duty to act as both the father and the mother of the good little citizens over whom they ruled and had influence.

To live up to their parental role, they also had to discipline the people to stamp out any behaviors they felt were bad or that had no place in a civilized society. Two men settling their differences between themselves in the form of a drunken brawl was deemed barbaric and outlawed. The state held the sole right to sanction any kind of violence, even though they alone would be the ones to dish it out should they feel it necessary.

The people were no longer allowed to take matters into their own hands when it came to retribution or exacting any form of justice for being wronged or cheated. They now had to plead their case to those in power and ask that their wrongs be made right, and it was at the discretion of those who knew best as to how or even if justice was served at all.

Fast-forward a few thousand years, and we find ourselves yet again being told that we do not possess the capacity to know what is best for ourselves and must behave like good little children to get a pat on the head. Any man who speaks or thinks for himself is now regarded as a barbarian who is unwelcome within the walls of the empire in its relentless pursuit of unification at any cost.

Any form of tribalism is now considered discriminatory or racist regardless of the fact that it is impossible to give an equal shit about everyone, everywhere. Within a tribe, every member is expected to pull his or her own weight and contribute to the strength and benefit of the tribe. Instead, we now have a collective push for a more socialistic way of life where everyone is expected to be given the same regard whether or not they contribute.

Earned is now a four-letter word and has been replaced with *deserve* in an effort to achieve fairness and equality. The merits of one's own actions now have little relevance to what he will receive as payment or compensation because there are those who either lack the ability, strength, or skill to perform the same tasks as others. Now the rewards must be divided equally among every-one in the spirit of equality, and any kind of discrimination is balked at and shunned by the new modern collective.

It should be noted here that throughout this book there will be references to *us*, *we*, and *them*. I've chosen the use of these words carefully and feel it essential to explain them before I go further. The words "we" and "us" when used with the word "col-lective" is referring to the falsely assumed wholeness of society. When used independently, it is referring to those on the outside of the empire that have chosen to reject the *we are the world* men-tality. The use of "them" is always used in reference to the out-sider and again those unwelcome within the empire.

It was important to explain the distinction and non-inter-changeable definitions of these words because, through habit in our everyday language, it has become far too easy to join the two. I do not regard each and every one of my fellow humans to be a part of my people. I am discriminatory.

I refuse to break bread, trade with, or live in harmony amongst those that, if given the opportunity, would take from me by any means necessary. Many times throughout this book the word *them* is referring to the U.S government and its politicians that claim to love and care about me when in reality, I am but a number or a vote in a ballot box.

The Declaration of Independence states that *all men are cre-ated equal*. While it's true that all human life has intrinsic value, it is still painfully obvious that some are more valuable than others and that not all life has value to everyone. The little refugee boy shown washed up on the shore after his people were denied immi-gration to a land not their own is not my problem, and unless you know or lived amongst that little boy, he isn't yours either.

You only think that you care about him because you were told to, and you do everything you're told by the elites. After all, the elites that sit in positions of power and authority believe they are the ones who know what's best for everyone else and must ensure that we all behave.

This kind of logic is hypocritical at best. It only moves the goal post for equality from the individual to the class. Oh yes, all men are created equal but only as long as they exist within the same respective class. Those in the middle or lower classes are not considered equals by those in power. The elites feel that we need for them to take on their paternal roles, and once again, we must be disciplined when we act out or misbehave. A sort of *rules for thee but not for me* system has been put in place to ensure that we all know our place.

Faced with all of this, it undoubtedly requires courage to make a choice to stand on your own two feet and become self-reliant. It takes courage to openly say that men are, in fact, not created equal. It requires courage to choose to be good at being a man, a husband, and a father. Refusing to allow the state to parent you and your children places a much heavier burden on your shoulders than those that simply wish to be guardians and allow the decisions made for your family to be dictated by the policymakers.

Make no mistake, those that choose this path are the modern barbarians in the eyes of the empire and are not welcome, but merely tolerated, for now. Post-modernists of the empire are the *good citizens* who have either decided willingly to submit or are only too blind to see that they have become subjects and slaves. To reject the diseased post-modernist culture of the empire where the murder of unborn children and the mass neutering of our young boys is celebrated with unbridled glee is all but a symbolic death sentence.

The courageous walk outside the walls relying only upon themselves while their tribes or families are looked upon with disgust by the more "civilized." How dare we spit in the face of their government-sponsored safety for the sake of our own sovereignty? How dare we choose not to be merely cattle but men who seek to be what we were born to be? How dare we choose to not live in fear but rather accept the risks that come with such a life. Not just merely an existence, but a life lived as it was meant to be.

At this very moment, masses of people are actively lobbying for their governments to take away the freedom of choice in the name of public safety. Their fear is now touted as virtuous, and anyone who is unafraid is being shamed for their courage. Those who have chosen to live as they see fit, get married, have children, start businesses, or simply reject the idea of unmitigated tolerance for depravity and debauchery are the new barbarians.

If the modern world is what passes for civilized, then we must possess the courage to have no part of it and build our nations and communities beyond the empires decaying walls. To live courageously today is to become your own master. This empire that you must reject is an empire of empty promises and filth that anyone with a pair of eyes that haven't been glazed over into a stupor by pornography and cheap entertainment can clearly see. To put it simply, to live courageously in the world today is to live rather than just exist.

None of these things are easy, and each one of them comes with its own set of risks and respective consequences, some greater than others. They make us afraid because of the unknown that comes after, but for men seeking to live with courage, the unknown must be met at full force and with a willingness to succeed and must not allow fear to deter them.

Men must still face these things head-on. We cannot refuse to live and be resigned to remain sitting on the sidelines of our own lives. There is nothing courageous about allowing life to happen *to* us. Courage can only be found when we acknowledge the risks and still push forward. We must not allow ourselves to be stopped. Choosing to live an intentional life that is free of false equality and superficial love is one of the hardest things we can do today because all other hardships have been taken from us by the blood and sweat spilled over the generations to create such a world.

Active living is accepting challenges and facing the possibility of defeat while caring deeply for your own people that you would actually give your life for. It isn't telling yourself that you are a citizen of the world and discarding your own interests for the sake of people who do not, will not, and absolutely cannot give a shit about you. To refuse mere existence and live, you must possess the will to face the consequences of living.

CHAPTER TWO
STRENGTH

"How does one become stronger? By deciding slowly; and by holding firmly to the decision once it is made. Everything else follows of itself."
— Friedrich Nietzsche, The Will to Power

If courage is to be measured by the presence of risk and fear, then strength is measured by the amount of resistance in direct opposition to another opposing force. And by no means will the act of leaving the comfort and relative safety of the empire be comfortable and not require a great deal of strength. Since the empire itself is no longer limited to the physical or a geographical location, leaving will require more than just packing up your shit and moving somewhere else because the empire is omnipresent. Anywhere you go, you will still find yourself within its walls.

As long as you remain within the walls of the empire, you will always be met with resistance. Since you can't physically leave, your exit must be internal, and as such, your strength must also be internal. Physical strength plays an integral part in the development of internal or mental strength, and your exit will undoubtedly require a great deal of both.

Throughout most of human history, strength has been a requirement to survive the harsh conditions in which people were forced to live daily. There was no choice to be weak because that was essentially choosing to die unless there was someone else with strength nearby to help keep you alive. Strength was required to procure food and shelter and ward off or kill raiders and bandits who were also strong. In those times, strength wasn't considered to be a virtue, but the average.

Today when you think of a strong man, the first thing that usually comes to mind is a massive bodybuilder who has transformed his body into that of a Greek god and can lift a seemingly inhuman amount of weight compared to others. Ripped muscles, a broad back, massive arms, and legs that look like tree trunks are now considered to be exceptional, whereas the average is further down on the other end of the spectrum in what our ancestors would consider either dead or soon to be.

No, not every one of our ancestors looked like Ronnie Coleman or Arnold Schwarzenegger. But on average, they did possess greater strength than the average man today, both physically and mentally. Thanks to their efforts, we can now afford a life where power is no longer a necessity for survival, and we can go through life as weak and as fragile as humanly possible due to the strength of other men and the government.

For most of us, we don't have to fight to secure our next meal. Even finding food today requires almost no strength at all as we can simply sit comfortably in a climate-controlled box that will take us as great a distance as necessary to a grocery store or market. There are no roving bands of bandits that we must be able to defend ourselves against should they decide to kill us and take what is ours. For most, we can depend on law enforcement and first responders to save us from a dire situation. In fact, we are now encouraged to let them handle it.

This resource provided by the empire is not likely to be going away any time soon; however, I've been wrong once or twice before in my life.

Strength out of necessity is merely a means to survive. But having strength purely for the sake of being strong is something else entirely. Because strength is no longer necessary in order to survive on a daily basis, possessing it is now considered virtuous and is often looked upon with both admiration and envy alike. Much like the ancient Romans held tests of strength between the gladiators in the great colosseum, we also now gather around to watch the strong compete for victory over one another as a form of entertainment and distraction from our otherwise uneventful lives while sucking down genetically altered chicken wings that the empire has so kindly provided.

So why then must we seek to become strong? If we have no desire to compete or entertain the masses and our physical needs for survival are being met, why then is it so important that we become stronger and more efficient men? The answer is because, without strength, no other virtues are possible to possess. You've heard the saying that the second amendment or the right to bear arms is what keeps the other amendments from disappearing altogether. It's much more challenging to take away someone's freedom when they have the capacity to hurt and kill you. You're welcome to try, but I would advise against it. Without strength, it would be impossible to possess courage, integrity, or discipline. You could even say that strength is *the* virtue.

In the modern world, nearly everything has been turned into a virtue. Are you really nice? You're virtuous. You pay your taxes on time? Virtuous. If you obey without question the laws set forth by your Omni-parent, the government, you are now considered virtuous. You are now even regarded as virtuous for being weak and afraid but somehow managing to make it through the day.

The word, strength, much like courage, has been so bastardized and subjugated to fit the modern narrative that everyone who ever does anything is somehow strong. That is except for those that are actually strong, of course. Those people are now considered privileged, and their accomplishments are all downplayed by the fact that they must have somehow had an unfair advantage in life that allowed them to get to where they are.

The *COEXIST* bumper stickers you see stuck to the back of every Prius driven by every female Harry Potter look-alike only apply to those who they consider to be the downtrodden or those who weren't born with some form of imagined privilege or another.

The weak are the ones whom they seek to coexist with because the strong have been made notorious for their propensity to be self-reliant while expecting others to be the same. Strength is another four-letter word to the empire and its subjects, but instead of being able to get rid of it altogether, they have changed the definition to suit their own purposes. The mere fact that the definition of strength has been accosted by so many that will perform whatever mind-bending mental gymnastics necessary to fit the bill is proof enough that strength is a trait that is still desired by all.

The irony in all of this is that while they perform these wild mental acrobatics, they are only making justifications for what they ashamedly are. Weak. Rather than taking it upon themselves to become strong and encourage others to do the same, they choose to dismiss any arguments that they aren't strong already. Social media and consumer marketing have enabled this line of thinking, more so now in the current age of *wokism* and body positivity. This *healthy at any size*, and you're perfect just the way you are mass marketing campaign has morbidly obese men and women believing their own lies that choosing weakness is a way of being strong.

This adoption has also come with a massive influx of people who have ever experienced a single emotion in their lives to self-diagnose themselves as being the victim of some form of mental illness or even imagining some form of oppression while simultaneously claiming that by embracing their victimhood, they are in fact strong.

Now let's be honest. We can all see that being physically and mentally strong is no longer necessary for survival in this new modern age, and those people who choose to remain weak and fragile will probably be just fine. Sure, there are more risks of disease and illness, but with the advantages of modern medicine, the citizens of the empire can still live a relatively safe existence for the most part. What is often overlooked is that choosing to remain weak is akin to a free man choosing to become a slave.

These *strong* victims of imagined oppression are the happy slaves of the empire. Their needs are met as long as they stay in line, never question authority, and report any and all violations of their own moral code to the jackbooted compliance officers that will swoop in to their rescue to ensure that their feelings are preserved—such happy slaves.

Slavery is one of those things today that you aren't supposed to talk about because it makes people uncomfortable, especially in the United States where there is a widely known history of slavery of African Americans in the south and the Chinese to the west where they were forced to labor the railroads in the name of progress. Although slavery, at least in the United States, ended with the American Civil War, slavery in the empire still exists to this day. But rather than physical, it is willful slavery of the hearts and minds with nearly everyone wearing the exact same set of shackles.

Thomas Jefferson, along with being one of the founding fathers of the United States, is famous for his quote, "*Malo periculosam, libertatem quam quitam servitutem.*" or "I prefer dangerous freedom over peaceful slavery.", a phrase that has been adopted by the flag-wavers who still hold a revolutionary view of how citizens of a republic should regard their government. However, there is still a large portion of the population that has chosen peaceful slavery because they lack the strength, both internally and externally, to endure a life of dangerous freedom.

They have chosen to live by the assurance that they will be kept safe, sheltered, and fed by their masters so as long as they don't make waves and obey like good little boys and girls. Good citizens of the empire. *Good.* These people will shame and mark any man or woman who does not share the same preference of subjugation as dangerous or toxic. Their exhibition of strength and courage is offensive to the soft, sugar-coated, weak minds and bodies of these modern slaves.

This feels unnatural to you because it is. You were not meant to be a slave that relies on the benevolence of a master for your safety and prosperity. You were meant for more. A man was evolved to fight, and hunt, and fill his own table and hearth with food and warmth. Your very nature cries out for a conflict in order to obtain the rich reward of safety. He was not meant to be pacified and nurtured throughout his life.

But how can he meet the call of his own biology in the world today? Most men today live a life that doesn't provide them with the need to hunt or fight in order to survive and take care of their family. The answer is simple. He must choose strength. He must choose the path of most resistance and discomfort.

Now in order to live as his body, mind, and even his soul were meant to, he must create his own conflicts and enemies. Yet, in this case, he only needs to accept that the empire is actually the benevolent dictator, the man behind the green curtain who's pulling the levers is his enemy. Once he has uncovered his enemy, he has a cause to rally behind. He has found his *them* and therefore can determine his *us*. It was always going to be *us vs. them* in the end. It only required that he choose which side of the line he was going to stand on.

Is he going to stand on the side of peaceful slavery? Or is he going to choose the tumultuous path of dangerous freedom and reject the hand that only waits for the slightest excuse to strike him down as an example to any others that may get the same idea? He absolutely must choose a side. There is no *middle of the road* for a man. The only things you can find in the middle of the road are the flattened rodents that were trapped by indecision and ended up splattered all over the pavement.

If he is to choose the path of dangerous freedom, he must sacrifice the luxury of safety. He must cut away the safety net and strike out on a quest to achieve something that can't be given to him by anyone but must be taken through his own will and effort. He must decide for himself what his own moral code of conduct is. Which laws he will willfully choose to ignore, thus making himself into an outlaw, a *skegamaor* that roams beyond the walls of the empire while still raiding its resources to provide for himself and his own clan. He must choose to become strong.

When a man chooses to become strong, he typically goes to the gym to lift weights, and if he's doing it right, he will ensure that he doesn't neglect any part of his body. That means he doesn't skip the dreaded leg day. However, physical strength means nothing without mental strength, and neither of them means anything without spiritual strength. A man is a sum of his parts, and since true strength is not built in a vacuum, he must make sure that he doesn't neglect any part of himself.

The act of starting with physical strength comes naturally to men. This is because there is a crossing over or bleeding effect that occurs when he is actively working to be stronger physically. Self-discipline is born from his efforts and commitment to the improvement of his body and, in turn, increases his mental strength and fortitude. *"Do hard things"* is a mantra that you will find in just about every single online self-improvement community and has become a common platitude that people will regurgitate at will, although many who won't look deeper into the concept itself.

Anyone who has spent any time under a barbell knows that his physical strength isn't all that improves during his workouts. The will and determination to get that one last rep can only come from his mind and his spirit. There is a disconnect between the body and the mind that is overlooked, whereas the two are more closely connected than many realize. In other words, a strong body will forge a strong mind. A rising tide lifts all ships, so the stronger one becomes, the more he can withstand and the more he can withstand, the more courageous he can afford to be.

In order to become physically stronger, a man has no other choice than to put forth continuous effort to do so. It cannot be accomplished passively or by accident. He must choose pain and discomfort and inconvenience as a form of bodily sacrifice to the gods in exchange for the gift of strength. The mental byproduct of this is discipline. Put plainly, discipline is simply the act of doing what must be done whether you are motivated to do it or not. Not relying on the superficial motivation that only strikes when he feels at his best, but deciding that his comfort and his feelings are inadequate excuses for failing to perform as necessary.

It is all too easy to skip the workout in exchange for sitting on the couch and living vicariously through other strong men while watching sports. The cost of this, however, is that you will ultimately remain weak. Today as I write this, the first name that comes to my mind when mental strength or toughness is mentioned is that of former Navy SEAL David Goggins. Goggins' mental toughness is all but legendary, but it was not something that came easy or natural to him. Just like going to the gym and lifting weights programs your body to become stronger, he had to program his own mind to become stronger.

In his book, Can't Hurt Me, he talks about how he had to brainwash himself in order to overcome the instinct to quit when things got hard.

"From then on, I brainwashed myself into craving discomfort. If it was raining, I would go run. Whenever it started snowing, my mind would say, Get your fucking running shoes on. Sometimes I wussed out and had to deal with it at the Accountability Mirror. But facing that mirror, facing myself, motivated me to fight through uncomfortable experiences, and, as a result, I became tougher. And being tough and resilient helped me meet my goals."

You only need to consistently perform a certain action or task about ten times in order for it to become a habit. By forcing himself to associate the things that were painful would make him uncomfortable as something that he simply must do, he was able to turn the act of displaying toughness into a habit where the side effect of all of this was that he became mentally tougher.

If there is a direct correlation between a strong body and a strong mind, then the inverse is also true. A weak mind will exist within a weak body, and a weak body will be the vessel for a weak mind; however, placing one's efforts solely into the strengthening of the mind will not affect the strength of the body. Sure, the stronger the mind becomes, the more likely it is for someone to come to the conclusion that he must also focus on his body, but this isn't necessarily the rule.

Discipline and mental strength come from intentionality and choosing of rewarding pain over comfortable pleasure. It comes from doing what has to be done and sacrificing one's own weakness and mediocrity to the flames in exchange for strength and exceptionalism. It is through accepting that there is no other way forward and making it non-negotiable. He must refuse to make compromises or excuses to himself because the only way to become mentally strong and more disciplined is to be mentally strong and more disciplined.

John Wayne once said, *"Life is tough, but it's tougher if you're stupid."* While intelligence is not something to be confused with mental strength, you aren't long for a life outside the empire if you don't know how to effectively navigate the world and the challenges it brings. There are plenty of smart people out there with weak minds. Intelligence isn't a measure of one's mental fortitude, rather only a measure of its aptitude for retaining knowledge and solving problems. But you should still work to not be stupid.

Again, strength is measured by the resistance it can withstand. Therefore, the amount of resistance that the mind can handle is a relation to its strength. In this age of wokism and equality, people have become not only physically weak but mentally as well. Any kind of thinking or ideas that go against a person's beliefs or somehow imply resistance is now all but criminalized and labeled as offensive.

Unlike our ancestors, who were just as mentally strong as they were physically due to it being necessary for their survival, having thick skin or a steady resolve has become unnecessary. The empire has seen fit to step in to protect you from experiencing any kind of shame or discomfort that could hurt your feelings and make you feel bad.

We can now afford to be just as mentally weak as we are physically because just like a mother will scold her child for picking on or making fun of a younger sibling, the empire will scold and correct anyone who simply states a fact if it hurts someone's feelings. If you haven't noticed already, the intervention of the empire has become something of a trend.

Things like promoting a healthy lifestyle through a good diet and exercise are now considered body shaming because a fat person could possibly somehow be reminded that they are indeed fat and unhealthy. Even now, the act of keeping your mouth shut and going to the gym to make yourself healthier and stronger is considered a form of shaming because someone else isn't doing the same thing.

The act of making money or achieving one's goal is now considered ableist or discarded as yet another product of privilege and goes against the modern ideals of equality. *If I can't do something, then you shouldn't be allowed to either.* Ultimately, if you fall anywhere above the average, you are a bigot and should be ostracized from our new bright and shiny society in the name of equality and fairness. Unsurprisingly, the ones who demand equality in all things are always the weakest.

With physical weakness being a form of slavery to the empire, mental and emotional weakness is slavery to oneself, and the only way to break free of the chains is to become stronger. We, humans, are still at our core being just animals. The only thing that separates us from the beasts outside of opposable thumbs is our ability to reason and rationalize. However, rationalizing is what has brought us here to an age of weakness. Since it is no longer required of us to be strong, we reason that it's ok to remain weak and give into creature comforts' desires.

As I stated before, you cannot just pick up and move somewhere to escape the empire because, again, *they* are everywhere. Your departure must take place internally rather than externally. You must possess the psychological fortitude to abandon their forced moral codes and realm of inclusiveness. You must possess the courage to face the consequences of being cast out and isolated, severing ties with the empty shell of protection that comes with being one of them.

CHAPTER THREE
BROTHERHOOD AND TRIBALISM

"NOW this is the Law of the Jungle —
as old and as true as the sky;
And the Wolf that shall keep it may prosper,
but the Wolf that shall break it must die.
As the creeper that girdles the tree-trunk
the Law runneth forward and back —
For the strength of the Pack is the Wolf, and
the strength of the Wolf is the Pack."
The Law of the Jungle
-Rudyard Kipling

However, unified the empire claims to be, there exists an epidemic of isolation, particularly among men. As anti-discriminatory rhetoric has taken the main stage, men's only spaces have become harder to find. This is a disturbing cultural and historical anomaly that has only recently occurred for thousands of years. The friendships and bonds between men have been revered by every great society.

As far back as the ancient Greeks, you can find extensively detailed accounts of brotherhood and tribe-like bonds between men that were celebrated, encouraged, and even envied. Aristotle even referred to a friend as a "second self," whereas now most male friendships today are superficial and proximity-based. This anomaly occurred when western culture shifted, and more and more women began to leave their home duties and transition into the workforce.

Before this shift occurred, males sought companionship with other men and developed bonds with them because there was no other choice. This shift also brought homosexuality to the light during the nineteenth and twentieth centuries. A rise in homophobia created a strain on platonic male friendships and made them suspect as homosexual relationships were then considered a major taboo.

The fear of being suspected of being a homosexual quickly brought a decline in male peer-to-peer friendships. Over time, this culture shift led to many men being left isolated and missing any real connection with other men. Shallow relationships took the place of those that were once deep.

As decades passed, this new definition of male friendship became the norm and quickly passed down to each subsequent generation. This is still typical today. Men need deep and emotional bonds with other men in order to thrive, yet it was a slight shift in culture that told them it was wrong. Because it was widely accepted, this new perception of male friendship and what it meant for masculinity was a lay-up for the empire that needed tribal-minded men to be more manageable.

Men were already being taught to believe that meaningful male friendships were indicative of homosexuality, so with the empires, unification strategy is was easy to enforce the idea that groups of male friends were even more homosexual. They divided these small tribes of men so that they could be more easily absorbed into the fold of the empire where unquestioned loyalty was demanded.

This newfound isolation left these tribal-minded men searching for something else to rely on and made them more willing to compromise on their beliefs and values in exchange for belonging to something bigger than themselves.

The empire retains its power over its subjects through isolation. While enforcing the idea that everyone belongs to everyone no matter their history, culture, or background, they create social islands on which each man exists in solitude. This politician-esqe double talk really means that you actually belong to no one if you belong to everyone.

In the second line of Kipling's poem, *And the Wolf that shall keep it may prosper, but the Wolf that shall break it must die.*, he is warning us of the dangers of being isolated and alone. While the risk of actual death isn't nearly as high as it is in a real jungle, there is a death, all the same, a slow and almost imperceptible one at that. The isolation that a man faces within the empire isn't just a physical one but also an emotional and spiritual one.

As the idea of tribalism has become taboo and the inclusion of everyone is encouraged more and more, a man's sense of belonging has waned. Does he truly belong to this new tribe of everyone? Is he supposed to see everyone as his brother? How is he supposed to love and care about everyone within the empire equally when he is just a nameless speck amongst the millions of people with which he shares no common ground?

A man's inability to connect with others in a real and meaningful way is a death sentence to his spirit. Just look into the eyes of a man that is living the stereotypical *American Dream.* He has a wife, kids, a house with a white picket fence, 30 years at a job, and a pension promise when he retires. What he doesn't have is anyone that he can call his brother—no tribe of men to which he had to earn his place in.

Look into those eyes, and you will find a deep void of longing and loneliness. The death of a man's spirit is a slow burn that eventually reduces him to all but a shell of the man he is meant to be. This means nothing to the empire. The empire only cares that he is tame and that he is kept occupied to not make trouble. He is but one of the million children that have been plopped down in front of the television and fed garbage and shallow entertainment. He is told that he is a citizen of the empire and that by creating this life, he contributes to the greater good of everyone.

He's been fucking lied to.

There are approximately 365 million people currently residing within the United States. Each of them with different values and moral codes. Where two people may or may not align, there will inevitably always be a third that goes against the grain. I started writing this book in January of 2021, nine months after the entire world was shut down due to the coronavirus. The powers that be decided that it was best for everyone to isolate themselves further, not only socially but physically and geographically, in an attempt to cull the spread of a virus with a 99%

survival rate.

Countless media outlets focused their efforts and attention on the perceived severity and morbidity of the virus. They began telling us all that we should all be afraid and shut ourselves off from the world. They continued to drive the narrative that if we didn't, we were all going to kill our grandmothers by spreading the virus to those that we love and strangers alike. Anyone who disagreed with or even doubted the nature of the threat was then set upon by the collective and publicly shamed. They were called ignorant, inconsiderate, and in many cases, *murderers.*

In what seemed to happen in less than one month, people who were once proud to stand upon their soapboxes, wave their flags, and tout just how much freer they were than everyone else suddenly began advocating for their own rights to be taken away. An empire that had already been politically divided by the 2016 presidential election was then divided even further. As the zealots on both sides of the aisle split again into splinter cells that consisted of the *morally righteous* who sought only to have everyone do as they are told and those who opted to take personal responsibility for their own health and safety.

Those morally righteous that had chosen fear as the newest and latest virtue fought back against free thinkers and anyone else who didn't toe-the-line and fall in step with the narrative put forth by the empire. When the narrative changed from "Please stop buying masks so that hospitals and their staff can get them." to "Everyone must wear a mask at all times whether indoors or out.", anyone not wearing a mask was treated like a pariah, the 21st-century leper who must be feared, shamed and banished from society.

Anyone not wearing a mask was a murderer, and lacked consideration for others, and was no longer welcome among the good, civilized people of the empire. They were right about one thing. With 365 million people in the United States, being expected to care for each and every one of them is both physically and biologically impossible. No one can possibly care about that many people at once. A person can't actually care about more than 100-150 people at any given time. Regardless of how many politicians shine their teeth from behind a podium and tell you that they care about each and every American citizen, it's biologically impossible.

We are all in this together.

That might sound good on paper and make you feel all warm and fuzzy inside, but in reality, it is nothing more than ideological pornography. It's a phrase intended to align the social islands you have been placed on in an archipelago of sorts to create the illusion of shared goals and values that matched that of the empire. We are not and have not ever been in this together. At least not since the empire's expansion rate increased to the point where everyone from everywhere was welcomed into the fold regardless of their beliefs and own cultural backgrounds and moral codes that came with them.

We have outgrown the chances of there ever being a *we*. A tribe of people can only remain a tribe as long as there is a sharing of values and a cause that everyone can rally behind. Once the tribe grows too large, an inevitable splitting will occur because people are just people.

They have such different ideas and morals that they will seek out others who possess the same. Once again, human nature and the desire for us vs. them takes over, and splinter cells begin to form within the tribe. When that happens, civil war is all but guaranteed as the opposing cells now find themselves at odds with one another and incapable of coexisting with anyone who isn't one of them.

Even the empire itself started to split as politicians across red and blue states made up their own minds. They decided that they would be the ones to determine if they adopted the extreme measures of isolation and lock their constituents down as prisoners of their own homes dictated by the empire or whether they enacted their own measures based on their constituents. Not that either mattered all that much to them, but the hope of getting re-elected swayed their choices.

They were nothing more than modern-day Constantines

who sought only the appeasement of their people to retain their power over them. This, of course, then split the constituents apart even further and set them against each other. More splinter cells formed, thus reducing the size of the tribe even further.

Almost two years ago, I was engaged in discussion with a peer on the subject of tribalism. He was a self-proclaimed socialist who dreamed of a utopian future where the *greater good* took precedence over the need for individual sovereignty and liberty. Like most socialists, he failed to take into account human nature as well as physics as a factor in the effectiveness and stability of this mythical land of milk and honey where everyone was equal, and no one desired or had the need to become better.

He laughed at my prediction that the nationalist rhetoric that was thought to have stemmed from the results of the 2016 election wasn't actually all that new and that it was only the next logical step of the devolution of the empire. Tribalism was slowly returning, but unlike the tribes of the past that were separated by geographical location, religion, or racial and ethnic differences' differing ideologies would be what caused the great divide.

The empire had grown too great and would share the same fate as the great tower of Babylon and crumble to the earth because the builders could no longer communicate with each other. The tower was meant to ascend to the gates of heaven itself, but it grew too great in measure and was then shattered to ruins. Again, not because they had built it too high, but because suddenly, those who worked to build it had become incapable of relating to each other.

A new fall of the tower of Babylon is what we see now in the current state of affairs in the modern world. In search of the heavens, the aspirations of one perfect world or nation have fallen victim to human nature. Like the people of Babylon were separated by language, we have become divided by values and ideologies. And like the people of Babylon, rather than finding common ground to continue to build, we found others that speak our language and formed tribes with them.

Unable to trust those that we simply cannot understand, we have set up our perimeters and marked our territories in an effort to defend ourselves and our tribe against *them*.

When I pressed him about the certainty of the people in this bright and shiny future becoming dissatisfied or restless, he simply swatted the idea down and an impossibility due to the lack of need for it. This seems to be a common trope among people within the empire. They have all but dismissed themselves from reality and the idea of nature by claiming to be *more evolved* or above it all in the sense of superior moral purity.

Nature has always had the last laugh, and she holds an impeccable batting average. In over a millennium of recorded human history, every rise, as well as the fall of an empire, has been predicated upon the existence and influence of nature, more specifically, human nature. The ancient Roman Empire fell swiftly to corruption, and the unrelenting assault of power grabs and coups with pride and arrogance almost always the driving force behind them. Man is incapable of acting against his own self-interests unless he genuinely loves something, and the thing that all men love more than anything else is power and the status that it brings.

The promise of power and status, especially over those that he does not see as either his equals or as part of his tribe, is a siren song that drives him to rise above others. No empire can stand indefinitely because of this. Outsiders being told that everyone has to regard them all as equals is nothing more than feel-good rhetoric that no man can take seriously. The lack of discrimination is what makes empires fragile.

If a chain is only as strong as its weakest link, then it isn't a stretch to say that an empire or society will only remain stable so long as the people's loyalty is never compromised. This means that the moral codes, ethics, and values are universally shared, and there is no desire to rise above one's station or position within the empire. If one or more of these are present, people will naturally gravitate towards others like themselves and cause dissent.

The desire to belong to something bigger than ourselves is

something that no man will ever be able to overcome regardless of his strength. We are social creatures, and it is only natural to be social with those we view to be like ourselves. Even the most ardent introverts are glued to their smartphones scrolling through social media apps interacting with and aligning themselves with other introverts.

But like the online introverts who seek out communities of people with the same views as themselves, everyone else is doing the same thing. It's not hard to figure out when you look at your own social circle and networks. There are people that you would never be able to work with or even be friends with because of how much their values differ from your own. Can you rely on someone to have your back in your time of need if their values are diametrically opposed to your own? Would you even risk it?

You couldn't and wouldn't because your own nature for self-preservation wouldn't allow it. You would seek out those that share your values. You would seek out a tribe. You will behave like Babylon's people and align yourself with those that you could understand and can relate to because you realize that there is no safety or security among those not like yourself.

The most effective and capable military units are almost always described as small and mobile. These are your SEAL Team 6's and other special forces units that can work together and maneuver without having to expend excessive amounts of energy and resources. They are, in every sense of the word, a tribe. Each member of these units is an extremely valuable individual because they possess a unique quality or skill set that they offer to strengthen the tribe.

By offering these qualities and skills to the strength and utility of the tribe, they increase their own value and are regarded as indispensable members of the team. Your own tribes and personal circles depend on this very same dynamic. The more you can offer the tribe, the more your tribe can provide you with. While it may sound like a cliche, Alexander Dumas aptly described this in his novel, The Three Musketeers. *All for one, and one for all.*

Being a member of a tribe or in-group requires discrimination if it hopes to survive. You simply cannot let just anyone in. D'artagnan wasn't just welcomed into the fold by Porthos, Athos, and Aramis without first being tested and evaluated to ensure that he would be able to pull his own weight and make the tribe stronger and that he shared the same values as they did. Anything less would be considered unacceptable, and he would not have been permitted to join the Musketeers' ranks utilizing discrimination based on merit.

This, while seeming perfectly natural and generally how most things are interpreted to be done even though the idea or mere mention of an exclusionary meritocracy has become antiquated and taboo in the modern empire's eyes. It suggests that someone will eventually be told that they aren't good enough based on specific characteristics or qualities that they either possess or lack, respectively.

This cannot be allowed by the empire because excluding someone implies the lack of loyalty to them, and the absence of loyalty to a citizen of the empire is considered an absence of loyalty to the empire itself. Anyone deemed by the empire to be disloyal is by default an enemy, and the empire refuses to tolerate dissent. Still, to become a useful and valued member of the tribe, you must be willing to abandon your loyalty to the empire and place it amongst your own people. Anything less is a half measure, and people who only perform half measures cannot be trusted to be relied on when they're needed.

A man must have the conviction to face the wrath and hatred of the empire for the sake of the tribe. He should pride himself on having beliefs that he refuses to abandon regardless of the possible consequences. Yes, there will be consequences. And there should be because without a cost attached, convictions and principles are worthless. This requires both courage and strength to withstand the consequences that will surely come his way when he decides to leave the empire.

The willingness to sacrifice a part of himself for the sake of the tribe is the final element that cements his place as one of them. And whether he has realized it yet or not, He wants to be one of them. He needs to belong to something bigger than himself but still small enough to know that his contributions matter. As Victor Frankl described it, this existential vacuum is only broken when a man knows that his life has meaning.

The empire tricks you into believing that you are a part of it while simultaneously painting romanticized pictures of the *lone wolf* archetype to keep you from finding your tribal brothers and becoming loyal to anyone else but the empire. This sets the stage for the nihilistic view of the world shared by far too many men leaving them in an existential crisis.

The lone wolf fallacy tells men that he is stronger alone and cannot be betrayed if he is a tribe of one. They make you feel good about yourself for becoming the isolated loner who repeats self-affirmations in the mirror, telling himself that *he who flies solo has the strongest wings*. The truth is that that being alone makes you more manageable. You can say to yourself that you'll be strong enough to withstand the tide of threats and influence of the empire and hold your ground like the Berserkir on Stamford Bridge, but this is nothing more than mental masturbation.

Yes, he showed great courage and strength as he fought off the Saxons, but in the end, they still killed him. He also had an army at his back that was maneuvering a retreat, and in the end, they still lost. That battle marked the ending of what we call the Viking age. An entire culture and way of life brought to a sudden halt by the empire who simply had more people. One man standing alone against the empire is no more a threat than an ant is to a grizzly bear.

And yes, while it is true that the Viking army still fell to the empire that day, they fell with one another and even with a sense of belonging to their own people. The empire was forced to amass an entire army against them because together, they were a threat that needed to be dealt with. The risk of being overrun and conquered was real to the empire, and they had no choice but to act. They saw the threat and were well aware of the risk involved with allowing the pagan tribe to go unchecked. Together they were strong and a force to be reckoned with. The courageous but lone Berserkir on the bridge was ultimately a minor inconvenience standing in the way of an army.

Then there still lies the fact that he wasn't alone at all. He belonged to a tribe, a clan, a united people behind a cause and common Gods that fought together side by side in the shield wall. Together they were stronger and capable of striking terror into the heart of the empire. He was no lone wolf by any stretch, and if you wish to survive beyond the pale outside the walls of the empire, you cannot be either.

Bare is the back of the brotherless man, for who is alone is nothing but a pliable subject that can be moved at will by a greater force. The empire wants you alone so much that the narrative has been changed to say that a man who is close with other men must be gay. The fear of being labeled a homosexual has kept many men isolated and alone, while his soul has cried out for a friend and brother to lean on.

A man needs his brothers. He needs the company of other men that he can measure himself against. In doing so, he is forced to face his own shortcomings, improve and grow more capable in his peers' eyes. He yearns for the respect and acceptance of other men because that solidifies his place within men's natural hierarchy. It quenches his thirst to belong to something bigger than himself that will value him in return in a reciprocal relationship. This something that he cannot find within a one-sided relationship with the empire.

He needs an equal measure of give and take with his brothers, and they need it from him as well. Obtaining another valuable member of the tribe makes them stronger and capable of acquiring new resources or withstanding an attack. It mutually benefits the tribe as well as the individual. This symbiotic relationship is in stark contrast to the parasitic relationship between men and the empire that feeds on the efforts of men to make itself stronger while giving nothing in return.

By becoming a tribal and exclusionary man, you are choosing to *unplug* yourself from the machine whose existence depends entirely on consuming your life force. Another metaphor described by the almost prophetic 1999 film The Matrix where the entirety of the human race save for a small group of rebels had been reduced to batteries that fueled the machines. You become more than just another cog in the machine, and more importantly, you can save your children from the same fate.

The power of the tribe comes from its members' strength, and by choosing your tribe over the empire, you become stronger. The similarities between the Viking shield wall and the Spartan phalanx are that each man must be strong enough to hold the shield to protect the man at his flank. Anyone incapable of this was unwelcome and, yes, discriminated against because to offer universal inclusion was to welcome the death and destruction of the tribe.

These weak and cowardly people suckling the empire's teat, these wretched masses that are happy to be ruled over as contented slaves, are not and should not be welcomed into your tribe. These *normal* people are not your equals. However, while you do not look at them as you do your tribe or even hold them in the same esteem, you also do not make the mistake of hating them. Hating them raises their worth to that of you and your own people, and they most certainly are not as equally valuable as your tribe.

I imagine that many who will read this book will find that much of what is said is politically incorrect or *hate speech*. They, of course, are not members of my tribe, and therefore I cannot hate them as I do not look upon them in the same regard as I do my own. It is impossible to hate that which warrants little more than pity and disdain. As a member of a tribe, you will find yourself with these same views.

You cannot hate those outside of your tribe because humanity itself is fragile, and one day your ranks will need to be replenished. If not the citizens of the empire who eventually make their own choice to cut the cord and stand under their own two feet, then by who? By hating outsiders, you limit your tribe's potential to grow stronger. The tribe that lives beyond the walls of the empire survives by raiding that empire for resources, and to a tribe and people are the greatest resource there is.

Caring deeply for your tribe while not caring one way or another for those outside your tribe is not the same as hating them. It is little more than indifference. The tribe cannot afford to hate the empire or its people, and doing so only expedites its own eventual destruction.

CHAPTER FOUR
LOYALTY

A man must be a friend
To his friend,
For himself and for the friend,
But no man must
Be a friend of a friend,
Of his foe.
-Havamal Stanza 43

The words of Odin contradict those imposed by the empire. Loyalty and friendship are not to be freely given to everyone but to those within your own tribe. The two primary tribes of the Norse gods, the Aesir and Vanir, brokered peace and held it because a war amongst the gods would only lead to the destruction of both tribes.

Leaving the empire isn't advocating for conflict or war, but a secession with conditions of peace. A man cannot be expected to be loyal and faithful to everyone for the sake of everyone. He lacks the capacity. However, through an act of loyalty to his tribe, he can agree to terms that uphold the peace between his tribe and the empire. This is in the best interest of those who are owed his loyalty and protection. A war between the tribe and the empire benefits neither and can only end one way. It is best to sue for peace rather than subscribe to one-sided loyalty.

The empire demands loyalty from the man in exchange for peace and protection, but this is not enough for the man. Man is bred to conquer, to war, to draw the perimeter around the fire that keeps his tribe warm and defend it against outsiders. This is a chosen loyalty, not one coerced or forced upon him by a crushing power from somewhere beyond the firelight. A chosen devotion is pure. It is given with the expectation of equivocal reciprocation, and it is valuable because it is indeed fragile. The empire is little more than a master to a horde of slaves that it will force to its knees if needed to retain order. Any loyalty afforded to it is shallow.

A man who is described as loyal comes with the implication that he holds strong support for something that he holds in high regard. Something that he at the very least sees as his equal. However, even a dog can be loyal to his master. After all, he is fed and cared for by this master while relying on his benevolence for safety and security. Even though he is often referred to as man's best friend, the harsh reality is that he is little more than property that holds its master in high but superficial esteem.

Having a sense of loyalty to the empire under the threat of punishment is like being little more than a dog. Yes, you're a good boy. *Here, have a treat. Just don't step out of line, or you'll be put down and replaced by a more obedient dog that knows its place.*

While this is true, what of loyalty to the tribe? Is it not the same as being a dog serving its master? It would be were it not for one small but important difference. To become a member of a tribe, you must first be loyal to yourself. Yes, the tribe is another collective that is greater than yourself, but you left the empire behind because you held yourself in higher regard. The very thought of forced loyalty left a bitter taste in your mouth, causing you to spit it back at an empirical master.

Before he can even make a choice to seek out or build a tribe of his own, a man comes to the determination that his decisions will be for his own benefit as well as others rather than just for others. He refuses to wear the leash while he remains in the yard like a *good boy* because going against his nature does not benefit him in any real way. His decision to seek out others like himself to join forces and share resources is predicated by his own personal loyalty. *If you want my help, there had better be something in it for me.*

Being interested in any way in your own self-preservation and benefit is taboo in the eyes of the empire. The idea of *the greater good* is spoon-fed to you through social programming at an early age, and you are taught to be loyal to your master. The master that feeds you keeps you safe and will lovingly whip you whenever it feels like you have forgotten just where you fall in the hierarchy.

The idea of being unquestionably loyal to the empire while being grateful for the beatings should grate against your very soul. You should not be content with being a slave or a dog that is nothing more than a number on a screen that has no choice but to pay never-ending tribute to his master. The very thought of this should turn your stomach and cause you to pull away, tear the leash, and go running into the untamed forests where true freedom and personal sovereignty is all that lies before you.

No different from how you cannot be connected to the empire and all of its people in any meaningful way, the empire cannot care about you in a meaningful way. Because of its scale, the empire can only look at you from above. It doesn't see *you*, rather an endless sea of nameless faces that, as long as they continue to survive, is evidence enough that it has fulfilled its only duty required. But the tribe, the tribe sees you. The tribe actually needs you just as much as you need it. This is a real symbiosis that creates a tangible benefit for both the man and the tribe and creates a relationship of real meaning and connection.

The tribe is the ancient and sacred forest that man is charged with protecting and preserving as he is provided shelter and warmth and food that is rewarded to him by that forest. Together, the two not only exist in harmony with one another but thrive because of their connection. A man can only honestly care for those who are close to him, both physically and spiritually. The tribe isn't some abstract idea of universal citizenship. He can see it, taste it, smell it, and touch it.

His fellow tribal members are his brothers and sisters, bound together by more than just blood. Like the terms strength and courage, the phrase, blood is thicker than water, has been misconstrued by modern bastardization, and, likely, you have never heard how it was meant to be interpreted. The phrase has either been shortened out of convenience or laziness from its original form. The original phrase is, *the blood of the covenant is thicker than the water of the womb*, meaning that to those you have sworn a covenant or blood oath to, you are bound to more so than those of your familial relations.

The brothers within your tribe may not share in your actual ancestral bloodline. Still, their commitment to you and yours to them is greater than the superficial assumption that you somehow *owe* your allegiance to someone simply because you're related to them. Allegiances aren't owed to those that do not benefit you. Allegiances are conditional. Take the American pledge of allegiance, for example. It is born of a great ideal but a flawed one. You're pledging an oath to a republic, but the republic is made up of people more than it is ideas. As it currently stands, most people of that republic are not one of your own and do not share the same values or beliefs as you. Pledging a meaningful oath to them goes against a man's best interests.

Often we see the comparison of our ancestors' morals and way of life compared to that of today. Our heroes of the past are now often demonized for violating current and modern values that, in their own time, were seen as normal and ordinary. This same fallacy applies to ideals once held to be great in the past. In the American Revolution, the colonists were a ragtag band of misfits seeking to break free from the chains of an empire that behaved very much the same as America does today.

The soon-to-be Americans then were more a tribe than they were a nation, and it wasn't all that difficult to get them all to band together behind a common cause. Save for a few loyalists who retained their loyalties to their empirical masters and the security that came with resisting any kind of change to the status quo, that is,

Today, America is among the ranks of the largest nations on the planet. The ideals of the tribe have all but vanished in a cloud of universal inclusion. America is now to the tribe as Christianity is to an ancient religion known only to the people born into it. In ancient times, to be of a particular faith meant that you were geographically and ethnically born into it. Most religions were exclusive to certain people while being exclusionary to everyone else. This, of course, changed with the introduction of Christianity.

To become a Christian, one needs only to profess his or her allegiance to the Christian God, say a prayer, and be baptized. Ultimately, the barrier to entry is pretty low. This is similar to the requirements needed to become an American citizen. Despite immigration laws and borders, becoming an American citizen is relatively easy as one only has to study for an exam, say the pledge of allegiance, and sign a few documents to be considered a citizen and be afforded all of the privileges and perks that come with it. There are no meaningful requirements that need to be met to become an American.

While a noble idea, the ease of becoming an American has worked against the original idea behind it. I can't say for sure whether or not our founding fathers lacked foresight or an understanding of human nature. Still, over the past 250 years or so since its birth, America has welcomed everyone, from everywhere, regardless of culture and values, merely expecting them to assimilate to the way of life here. Again, this is a noble idea, but foolhardy when you neglect the harsh reality of people's nature in general.

Identity is everything to a man, and that identity must be meaningful and tangible. The broad interpretation of being an American no longer means what it did when that group of brave men gathered together in secret to draft and sign The Declaration of Independence. American identity has now been morphed into that of the Iroquois, a confederation of Native American tribes that joined together to create a new and much larger tribe. But even they eventually fell to the differences that they were so willingly importing into their new nation.

Tribal and individual identity must remain small to retain any kind of meaning. Yet as a member of the empire, man's identity is erased and soon loses all of its meaning. It becomes just another buzzword used by the media and political elites to inspire some surface-level emotion about belonging and unity. By way of the need to belong to a particular group, human nature has given birth to our current age of intersectionality. This isn't necessarily a bad thing on its own, but there is a caveat like most things within the empire.

There is a double standard bent in such a way as to disadvantage and handicap those whose values and moral compass do not align with that of the empire. While social categorization by race, creed, ethnicity, class, and gender is taboo and viewed as harbingers of interdependent discrimination systems, anyone not subscribed to certain idealogues is now demonized.

It's okay to identify as a member of a tribe so as long as it's not the wrong one. Any group that has ever been considered disadvantaged or oppressed is encouraged to retain their tribal identity while everyone else is excluded from this. They are expected to apologize and flagellate themselves for belonging to any group that has ever been seen as in a position of power.

The western man is now regarded as a pariah who must make amends for any Westerner's sins that have ever done anything viewed as wrong or politically incorrect. If he refuses, the empire will simply shuffle the deck, pull a random card, and assign them the label of one -ism or another regardless of whether or not he himself has ever committed any act that would warrant such a designation. He must now bend the knee and subjugate himself to every other tribe but his own and discard any shred of his own personal identity.

For example, anyone who isn't a complete piece of garbage can quickly come to the determination that racism of any kind shouldn't be tolerated. Still, today we are told that it is no longer enough to just not be racist. One must now adopt the new identity of being anti-racist and become a self-deprecating flag-waver for social justice and self-guilt if his own tribe has ever done anything to anyone that someone didn't like.

This forced loyalty is no different than the forced loyalty of a slave to his master. It's shallow and meaningless and meant only as a way to deter the lash of the whip. These conditions are nothing more than masturbatory theatrics meant to appease the empire's fallacy of equality for all through forced empathy and bowing.

Make no mistake that this is identity theft in its most literal interpretation of the phrase. The empire now stands as the moral authority of which identities are approved and which ones aren't. Even then, those identities are forbidden along with any exclusionary practices unless authorized by the elites that know what's best for you better than you.

The word Brotherhood has also been watered down to the point of nothing. As a man, you are expected to throw away your own self and tribal identities with any sense of exclusive belonging. Put simply, you are only allowed to be who you're told to be, and you belong to no one but also everyone as part of a conditionless relationship with universal inclusionism.

But by belonging to a tribe of brothers with whom you have sworn a covenant, your individual identity becomes a part of the tribe that remains meaningful, both to you and the tribe alike. The word Brotherhood retains its original meaning. It remains a conditional bond between those within the tribe, and should those conditions not be met, order is then enforced, and the violating member of the tribe is then cast out and ostracized.

True Brotherhood and loyalty are and should be exclusionary. It is a ridiculous concept that everyone and everything should be tolerated, but that is precisely what this age of intersectionality has brought us. Rather than shunning those whose morals and values do not align with our own, we have to now throw on our best pair of mental sweatpants and perform every conceivable gymnastic to *see things from everyone else's point of view*.

We are expected to excuse any forms of depravity and debauchery as simply *cultural differences* that must be understood and accepted. In not doing so, we risk someone feeling left out of the group. Many western European countries are prime examples of this. With the influx of mass immigration from third-world countries, rape has become the most common occurring crime. Rather than rejecting this and calling it what it is, the people there are told to accept it as a new and more inclusive cultural norm.

"Welcome to the new cultural exchange. I'll be your rapist today, and you have to bend over and accept it because it's just how things are done where I'm from. If you don't, I'll do it anyway because your masters have already accepted it on your behalf."

All this is the name of *tolerance.*

This has spread to the United States and can be seen on every television screen in every home as soon as one member of a minority group is killed by law enforcement. Regardless of the circumstances, this will result in mass riots. Riots where the homes and businesses of those who had absolutely nothing to do with the incident are looted and burned for so-called *justice.* Any kind of disavowing of these criminal acts is out of the question. Instead, the empire will begin its routine of justifying them as *feelings* or *built-up anger from years of blah blah blah.*

This is why you have insurance, they say. Or, *the wanton destruction of your home and business pales in comparison to the tragic loss of life of the rapist/murderer at the hands of law enforcement; therefore, you should accept it or be labeled as a racist and xenophobic asshole.*

Ironically, this pulling of the pendulum will only last for so long before it swings the other way, and chaos will ensue.

The thread was already pulled loose, and the tapestry is already starting to unravel. It's only a matter of time before the empire decides that any identity other than that of those who resign themselves to being happy slaves will be taken, regardless of culture or ethnic background. That's right. No one is safe from the chopping block once the elite has decided to do away with them once and for all. Even if you belong to a minority or culture catered to today, they will eventually come for you too, and there is nothing you can do about it.

The only hope you can have is to belong to a tribe of others like yourself who have left the empire and are loyal only to their own. This does not mean that there is no risk to this. A tribe must be discerning about who it allows in and should be discriminative of the nature or background of its members. Allowing someone who does not share the same values and allegiances can lead to the destruction of the entire tribe.

As I stated above, loyalty and brotherhood are conditional, and should those conditions be unmet, the act of betrayal is a real possibility. In the Poetic Edda, the story of the trickster god Loki's betrayal of Baldur, Odin's favorite son, is a lesson in this. Contrary to pop culture entertainment, Loki was not the brother of Thor but actually the son of a *jötunn*, or giant named Fárbauti, whose name means *cruel striker.* The jötunn were another tribe that was always warring with the Aesir and Vanir, the two chief tribes of gods that resided in Asgard.

It began when Baldur began having dreams of his own death that he had shared with his mother, Frigg. Odin the All-father sought answers to this and consulted the *völva,* whom he had summoned from the dead. After they confirmed that Baldur would indeed die, Frigg demanded a pledge be made by all things in existence that they would never harm her son. All but mistletoe made this pledge which was reasoned to be so harmless that Frigg never gave it another thought as Baldur was one of the mightiest of the gods.

Loki learned of this and concocted a plot against Baldur. He fashioned a spear made of mistletoe and tricked Hodr, another son of Odin, who was also blind to throw the spear at Baldur as a joke while Baldur boasted of his newfound indestructibility. The spear pierced Baldur's heart, killing him instantly. Hodr was punished and killed for his crime while Loki was banished to torture that would last until Ragnarok, the end of days.

One single betrayal would lead to the complete destruction of the gods. Not only did the tribe lose Baldur, one of the mightiest gods of all, but they also lost Hodr. All this from a single betrayal. Loki's nature was that of a trickster and one whose loyalty was questionable. He belonged to the enemy of Asgard from the very beginning, and it was his natural allegiance to them that destroyed everything.

This tale warns us of being too trusting of outsiders and those not like ourselves. Even when done so for the sake of peace, it is sometimes best to retain reservation and a certain level of suspicion of those who come from tribes with values not like our own. Today, the empire will call this natural instinct for self-preservation racism or xenophobia because we must accept everyone from everywhere and write off our differences that could weaken us as strengths.

While not every who is not like ourselves will bring about the destruction of our tribe, just like not every jötunn betrayed the Aesir, to believe that everyone is benevolent and means us no harm is foolish. Stereotypes exist for a reason. Not all of them apply to everyone but exist as a general rule to be aware of. It's even more foolish to deny that we all have, acknowledge, and even take them into account when dealing with people that we don't know.

Think of a dog whose only experience with people has been one where he is beaten and abused. Naturally, he will conclude that humans mean to do him harm, and he will regard all of them as dangerous beings that are not to be trusted. It takes strength and courage for him to even be willing to let his guard down enough and trust a human enough to let him get close, but he will still be suspicious of them.

We have seen what people are capable of. The news media is a constant barrage of examples of the worst. Why then, with so much evidence to the contrary, should we blindly accept everyone as one of our own? While it is counterproductive to loop everyone into the same group, not recognizing that some people cannot and should not ever be allowed within our perimeter to threaten the safety of our tribe is natural and needed to survive.

It isn't racism to see an African American man dressed in what we know to be thug-like clothes standing on a corner in an urban environment and instinctually become cautious and distrusting any more than it is racism to see a white male with a confederate flag t-shirt and assume that he himself may, in fact, be a violent racist against African Americans or anyone who isn't white for that matter. However, these thoughts and instincts for self-preservation are demonized by the empire and regarded as unwelcome within their society. As a man, it is your duty to protect and provide for your tribe, and to do so, you must use every ounce of evidence, every experience, and every tool at your disposal.

The empire condemns this because they hold the monopoly on your safety and security. They will regard everything you do for your own benefit or that of the tribe as you spitting in their face and undermining their ability to keep you safe. You are expected to deny your own nature and biological role as a protector.

This is what makes you a man! You were born to stand at the edge of the firelight, peering into the darkness in search of threats to your tribe and family. You were born to take action and make decisions about your own safety, yet the elites look upon you as merely a child that should pledge both its life and loyalty to the empire and accept any risks *as just one of those things* that happen.

A man's loyalty is owed to first himself and then to his tribe. An empire that is not willing to allow a man to protect his own is owed nothing. Although universal globalism sounds good in theory, the reality is that it has murdered a tribal culture. While some may argue that this is a good thing, the destruction of any culture is always a tragedy. The empire, simultaneously pushing for everyone to be themselves and the unbridled tolerance of everyone's differences is in direct defiance of man's true nature.

It erases the boundary lines between different cultures and tribes and removes the ability to discriminate against one another. As I have already said, discrimination is, in fact, a good thing, and not everything or everyone should be tolerated. We need borders and enforceable boundaries. Why do we feel the most in our natural state when we are with those like us? Because we are a part of something bigger that acts as an extension of who we are.

Refuse to be discriminating with your loyalty, and you will soon find yourself surrounded and unable to determine your tribe and those who seek your destruction.

CHAPTER FIVE
HONOR

Deyr fé,
deyja frændr,
deyr sjalfr it sama,
en orðstírr
deyr aldregi,
hveim er sér góðan getr.

Deyr fé,
deyja frændr,
deyr sjalfr it sama,
ek veit einn,
at aldrei deyr:
dómr um dauðan hvern.
- *Havamal Stanza 77 (Nynorsk Translation)*

Cattle die,
Friends die,
So, too, must you die.
Though one thing
Never dies;
The fair fame one has earned.

Cattle die,
Friends die,
So, too, must you die.
I know one,
That never dies;
Judgement of a dead man's life.

The Famous Greek hero Achilles boasted that his name would be spoken for thousands of years after his death because of the life that he lived in pursuit of a reputation worthy of being remembered. The poem above found within the Havamal is talking about honor, or as Achilles referred to it, reputation, as being immortal. Your wealth will one day dry up, your relatives and friends will one day return to dust, but the reputation and honor earned by a man throughout his life are everlasting. The counter stops on the day he dies, and the reputation that he built up to that point is locked in. Nothing can be added or taken away at that point.

Throughout your life, you have the opportunity to make decisions. The decisions will affect your reputation in one way or another, but as long as you are still alive, you can continue to make decisions to change or improve your reputation. It's when you die that your reputation is sealed forever. Whether you lived a life where virtue meant very little to you, or if you lived an honorable life, the ability to change one's reputation disappears on the day he dies.

Everything that you did up to that point is what will be remembered. Your reputation, the esteem afforded to you by your peers, your honor will be etched into the stones of time for all to see. Will you be remembered as an honorable man? Will you be remembered at all? The actions you take in this life will answer these questions far more accurately than your words.

If you are satisfied with dying and being forgotten, or worse, being remembered as a man of low character or honor, then you wouldn't have bought this book. You wouldn't have spent the last four chapters swearing under your breath because you were being told the truth for the first time.

But suppose you, like Achilles, seek to be remembered by your peers and your life celebrated by your descendants as the one example that they must all strive to emulate within their own lives. In that case, you must dismiss the empire's definition of honor and seek immortality by becoming genuinely honorable.

What does it mean to be an honorable man or to have honor? At its most base definition, honor is regarded as both an act as well as a virtue that has been inextricably tied to esteem and deference between men within a particular group or culture. To be honorable is to be considered worthy of the respect and admiration of men. In the latter case, having honor simply means that you have a reputation for *being* honorable by unfailingly adhering to specific codes of conduct within your tribe.

Across multiple cultures, honor can mean something different as each one will naturally possess its own unique codes of conduct. Because of these variances, honor is something that is romanticized by men of nearly every background. The *bro code* in modern western culture is one example of an honor code accepted by a particular culture or tribe. But if you've been paying attention to this book, you are already acutely aware that modern western culture has become corrupted with iniquity and the universal acceptance of all.

Within the walls of the empire, those with the most power and influence are afforded the privilege to define themselves and their behaviors as honorable, setting the standard for its subject to abide by. The issue with this is that the empire's hierarchical structure affords power and influence not necessarily to the honorable but to the wealthiest and most popular regardless of character virtues.

The old saying, *might is right,* is just a way of saying big fucks small. And if you can fuck it, you own it. If you own it, you have power over it. And if you have power over something, you can impose your own will and codes of behavior on it. The ones with the most power get to determine what is worthy of honor for those beneath them, and those currently in power have deemed their own corruption of your soul as honorable.

A code of honor is a system dependent upon the setting and following of ethical rules and principles. These act to govern a society based on shared ideals that define what is or isn't aligned with the morals and values within that particular society. This is often described as *Cultural Honor.*

In all its power and influence, the empire is ruled by men who have decided that you must abide by the codes of conduct that they have deemed fit for a universally inclusive society. This grand experiment, this melting pot of ideas, has shown that not all alchemy is sound alchemy. Some materials, when combined with others, can create the sharpest of blades. In contrast, other combinations weaken it, and we have, in fact, grown weaker and dishonorable as we have grown in the diversity of morals.

This does not sit well with men because their honor is measured by the esteem and respect given to them by their peers, but this is only possible if their peers share the same standards for what is considered honorable. If there is no uniform code of conduct, no standards to be upheld, then the pursuit of an honorable life is all but impossible should a man remain tethered to an empire where values and moral codes are not shared by everyone.

A man should care very little if the empire itself sees him as honorable. As mentioned in the previous chapters, the modern empire has taken strength, courage, brotherhood, and loyalty and twisted them into perverse codes that only further the rancid devolution of its subjects' character.

Because the empire's own code of conduct has been corrupted by humanist universalism, a tribal man's hunger for honor is only made more significant. This explains why he longs for strength and courage and is drawn to the loyalty that comes with belonging to a tribe of his peers. Man's need to measure himself against the mettle of other men and prove himself worthy of honor is fueled by the empires unnatural redefining of these virtues.

The empire has retaliated against man's hunger for honor by way of cheap entertainment and the display of insipid individuals willing to whore themselves out on camera to millions in exchange for monetary gain in the form of reality television. Their willingness to degrade themselves in a fervent race to bottom has captured honor and held it hostage.

The stories of our heroes have been replaced by real housewives living their 600-pound lives. Cheap circus acts meant to distract man from searching for fulfillment and honor by injecting poison straight into his soul. Rewarded with fame and adoration, these people inflict their influence on our children, corrupting them as we must leave them sat in front of a screen as we venture out and tend the proverbial salt mines for the good of the empire's expansion.

These people have all resigned themselves to be remembered as pathetic laughingstocks, like circus freaks whose end is perpetuated by the citizen-cattle feeding at the trough. The masses that adopted this nihilistic point of view that they themselves have no meaning in the end. They have no intention to leave behind a legacy that will echo across both time and space, with their name being spoken in reverence by those that follow them.

Where then are we to look for honor? Amongst our peers? Our peers have pledged their allegiance to the empire and adopted the moral code of the depraved. To seek honor and to be honored among them is to sacrifice our dignity and self-respect. Their code is not of their own volition but that of the empires. To stand as his own sovereign, a man must choose his own code that will uphold the standard of conduct demanded of those within his tribe.

It must be meaningful and exclusive. It should require a sacrifice of his most basic self as ideals quickly adopted are most often shallow. He must decide for himself what is moral and just. Not just in only what is considered legal by the empire but just in a way that he can look at himself in the mirror without feeling shame or a loss of personal pride.

I emphasize *just* over legal because the word justice has joined the ranks of those that have been perverted and changed. It is now used in a way to suit only those that subscribe to the same corrupt code held by those in power. Today, many laws only promise justice to those with power and influence while discarding anyone else. This affluence holds sway over the distribution of empirical justice.

Those lacking in true honor but in possession of power and influence have a different set of rules than everyone else. Classism is ironic in a system said to be equivocal. But it isn't fairness or the absence of it that drives the wedge between justice and injustice. It is the conflagration of justice and the morally superior by a society that at its own discretion is directed by the loudest and most ethically corrupt.

A man must allow himself to be stepped on and insulted by others so long as it doesn't result in damage to the empire. Any act of upholding his honor and reputation will be met with force at the hands of the empire that has decided that it is the sole keeper of power and only it can determine what is tolerated and what isn't.

If a man is incapable or not allowed to uphold his honor, then his honor is meaningless. To preserve his own soul, a man must have the conviction to maintain it regardless of the looming threat of the empire. He must be willing to defend and uphold that code of honor by facing the wrath and indignation of those within the empire by drawing a line in the sand and holding it with everything he has.

You become what you tolerate.

I first heard those words a few years ago while listening to a podcast to drown out the noise of my coworkers as they prattled on about their lives and incorrigible behaviors. Each of them attempting to one-up the other in a race to see who held the title for most morally corrupt, a living example of the empire's lack of an honor code.

If you become what you tolerate, you must become less tolerant in a society that will go out of its way to press its ideals. The ideals that all are equal in worth, regardless of who or what they are and what they bring to the table. You must not be universally tolerant, or you will eventually become one of the soulless hordes marching towards its own inevitable destruction.

The only hope of seeking honor and living an honorable life is by leaving the empire and swearing allegiance to yourself and a tribe of well-vetted individuals that have come to this same conclusion. You must abandon the cold and sterile fluorescent lights of the soulless empire and seek refuge within the raging fire of the tribal circle.

Within the firelight of the tribe, there exists the possibility of real and meaningful honor in all of its intended forms. Not just cultural honor, but reflexive, horizontal, and vertical honor as well. While the empire is satisfied with its own established cultural honor, to exist outside the realm within the interconnected workings of a tribe, a man must be able to uphold all other forms of honor as well.

Reflexive Honor can be described as an instinctive desire to *save face* or uphold one's reputation amongst his peers. This is most accurately described as, "If that guy punches me in the face, I'm going to punch him in the face." By refusing to allow himself to be struck with impunity, a man spits in the face of the empire who demands that it alone has the authority to distribute justice. By exuding reflexive honor, a man draws a line in the sand that cannot be crossed without consequence.

His tribe will only accept those willing to defend the perimeter and strike back when it is accosted or threatened. By doing this, a man establishes and upholds his reputation as one that will not simply be walked on or betrayed without at the very least putting up some sort of a fight. This makes him valuable to the tribe but a threat to the empire who will crush the man whenever it feels necessary to do so for lack of fear of any reprisal at all. The empire's worth, after all, is measured in part by those that fear and respect its power. Man's worth within the tribe is the same.

When those who fear or respect their power and possess their own sense of reflexive honor and fearsome power coexist within a tribe, this is called *Horizontal Honor*. Horizontal honor the mutual affording of respect and esteem between peers and those of equal status within an exclusive and discriminating community. This mutual respect isn't to be confused with tolerance of everything as it is so often done within the empire.

It must be earned by proving one's worth to the tribe through the acts of strength and courage, and loyalty to the tribe. There must exist an unyielding adherence to the standards and code of honor within the tribe to earn this horizontal recognition of honor. Equally, there must exist the possibility and threat of ostracization from the tribe should one fail to meet the standards set forth and expected of each and every member.

This is a zero-sum equation. There is no nuance, nor is there left any room for it. You are either held in a position of honor amongst your peers, or you bring dishonor to both yourself and the tribe and must be excommunicated. There is no participation trophy for doing one's best. You aren't special here, and if you cannot measure up, you are not good enough and must face the consequences of your own failure.

Horizontal honor is the receipt that you are given upon paying the price of admission. There are no discounts, and there are no deals. The price must be paid in full.

In addition to horizontal honor within the tribe, Vertical honor is the act of bestowing honor to those that are more superior in skill or rank within the tribe. It is a product of meritocracy where the best are rewarded for being the best and are owed more respect and esteem than the other members. Think, tribal chieftain or leader. Unless you are counted among the celebrity or political elite, it is impossible to earn vertical honor within the empire. Within those walls, everyone is regarded as equally useless nothings.

Within the walls of the empire, a more superficial version of vertical honor is given to those with fame, political power, and influence. Sure, there are a few exceptions to the rule, but for the most part, the individuals mentioned above have done nothing to earn their place outside of pretending to be something they're not. Teenagers with zero accomplishments and whores on YouTube are now called *influencers.* By its very definition, an influencer has the power to affect the decisions and thinking of other people from a position of authority. What authority?

The so-called power that these individuals have is nothing more than the ability to garner attention. For the most part, that attention is afforded to them by whining, self-depreciation, and spouting victimhood rhetoric to millions of people online. They have no real-life experience. They have won no hard-fought battles on or off the literal battlefield and have never been faced with any real adversity. It is ridiculous to think that these people have any influence over anyone, yet here we are.

But outside of the walls of the empire, power, influence,

and vertical honor are held for only those who have proven themselves and who possess a mastery of both themselves as well as skill. They had to earn their honor with merit by first paying the price of admission to the tribe in full as a baseline criterion. They are worthy of vertical honor because they first met the requirements for horizontal honor. There was no privilege or luck involved in this. They had to earn their position.

Within the tribe, vertical honor cannot be attained if horizontal honor isn't present. These modern influencers have done nothing worthwhile to earn your mutual respect, much less be elevated to a station above you. Their fame means little when it wasn't earned first from their peers with whom there is mutual respect between them, and these useless nothings are not your peers. The same applies within a tribe or honor group. No one becomes chief or leader without first earning their place as a peer and then stepping it up a notch further.

Ultimately, your honor is your reputation that is earned amongst your equals. If you choose to reside within the empire, everyone is your equal, you are all at the bottom, and frankly, your reputation is worthless. There is no greatness at the bottom, but any attempt to rise above the muck will not be rewarded with honor but with shame from your peers. This *crabs-in-a-bucket* mentality compels them to pull anyone who attempts to elevate their station back down with them because it exemplifies their own lack of achievement.

Think about it. The last time you tried to accomplish something that was above and beyond your peers' minimum expectations, 9/10 of them didn't offer encouragement but rather bombarded you with reasons why you shouldn't even make an attempt in the first place. It's because your own growth will leave them behind and place you above them on the food chain. By increasing your own value, you shine a spotlight on theirs, and it makes them uncomfortable.

"Oh, you think you're better than me?" Well, pal, if you even had to ask that question, the answer is clear that *you* think that I'm better than you.

As a man, you are hardwired to attempt to conquer, excel, and achieve more than what you are just given. It's only the pressure and guilt-trip tactics of your peers that hold you back. Having the strength and the courage to dismiss them while relentlessly pushing forward is going to make them abandon you, and that's okay. You don't need their permission or their approval to rise.

If they are content to remain bottom feeders vying for table scraps, then that is on them. You have no responsibility to those that do not wish to help themselves and put forth the same effort and commitment regardless of how many times the empire forces the idea that you owe everyone something down your throat.

This is the price of your personal honor. You cannot deny yourself honor for the sake of others' feelings. They must seek out their own path to honor, and while you can become the lighthouse beacon that shows them the way, you cannot drag them behind you. The empire expects you to limit your own strength and potential as a man and tries to shame you into submission. They call your quest for personal honor toxic and dangerous.

They are only half right. There is nothing toxic about men striving to be better at being men instead of being a good man by the standards of the empire. There is nothing toxic about becoming better than the bottom feeders. There is nothing toxic about having zero regards whatsoever for how uncomfortable your own progression makes people feel. If they feel weaker because you become stronger, then it is their responsibility to make themselves stronger. If they either can't or flat out refuse, then fuck them.

The part that the empire did get right is that your quest for honor is, in fact, dangerous. Not to your peers, but to the empire itself. They wish to keep a monopoly on strength because if they don't, and their subjects become too strong or too independent, their own authority and influence are weakened. They don't want you to rise above your station because you become much more difficult to manage in doing so.

Fuck that. You, as a man, were not meant to be managed and controlled by those with less merit than your own. Imagine cattle leading humans to the slaughterhouse. It's ridiculous, but that is exactly the dynamic the empire wishes to maintain. Strong, honorable, and free-thinking men who do not need to depend on the empire for survival and cast loyalty to their own tribe are a threat to the empire's existence.

Good.

If the empire wants to be afforded vertical honor from you, then they had damn well better earn it because as an honorable man, your respect and esteem are not given freely. They must be earned.

CHAPTER SIX
STRUCTURAL INTEGRITY

*"We are realities in a real world, and we must accept the reality
of our nature and all its thrillableness if we are to live in accord
with the real world, and those who try to get away from these
realities, who by ukase of the will deny their existence, succeed
only in living in a world of illusion and misunderstanding."*
— Jack London; "Pugilism is an Instinctive Passion of
Our Race," *Dallas Times Herald,* July 17, 1910

*"He was a killer, a thing that preyed, living on the things that lived, un-
aided, alone, by virtue of his own strength and prowess, surviving tri-
umphantly in a hostile environment where only the strong survive."*
—Jack London; *The Call of the Wild,* Chapter VII

The ancient Greek philosophers can be accredited for much of the cliche wisdom that is shared today. Still, their takes on life and man's nature have either been skewed by modern society or were skewed themselves by their tame and civilized nature that was undoubtedly a product of their culture's rapid advancement. There is an *un-wildness* to them. They sought more to tame the beast within man rather than to foster their own nature as a means of becoming more of who they truly are.

It has been said that a man is the average of the five people that he spends the most time with. While there is truth in that statement, it leaves out an essential factor in what makes up a man. A man is the sum of his habits and actions carried out in the dark. He is the sum of many moving parts that should one be denied, the others will wither. His integrity speaks to his honor, and a lack of it speaks to the sincerity of his honor.

The most common definition of integrity is the habit of doing what is right and honorable whether you are being watched or not, but the integrity of a man is much more than that. When you think of structural integrity, you consider how well put together something is. For a man to possess structural integrity, he must be whole and undivided and sovereign. He must have the strength to withstand the pressures of outside forces that, left unchecked, would bring him crashing down.

The Latin root of the word actually derives from the words for wholeness or intact-ness and integration. In this case, the word integration is not to be confused with assimilation. It means the complete and undivided integration of all of a man's parts, the parts that, when put together, create a man as he should be. To live a life of honor, a life lived in the shadows must be consistent with a life lived in the light. This rings truer to the more modern and most commonly accepted definition of integrity.

Along with the other perversions of the empire, the definition of men and young boys alike has been twisted to simply mean *broken girl*. Men and boys are regarded as one-dimensional and possessing only one purpose or use to the empire. That use is but to protect the walls of the empire whenever called upon but in the interim are expected to reduce themselves to the docile nature of the feminine. Men are seen as but a tool locked behind glass with a sign that reads, "Break only in case of emergency."

Any act of manliness or display of one masculinity is considered inconsistent with the needs and temperament of a polite society that has no need for such things outside of extreme situations. But a man is not one-dimensional. As I said before, a man is the sum of many parts and is only a complete version of himself when all of his elements are maintained and utilized as they are intended to be by nature.

The empire has no use for a complete man as the elements that make the man are outsourced by the empire and assigned to the governing state. A complete man is a threat and considered dangerous. He is the wayward boy that must be disciplined and reigned in by his masters as he chomps as his bit and pulls at his chains waiting to be cut loose. He is the pacing lion in the cage that longs to feel the heat of the savanna on his feet and the wind rushing through his mane as he hunts. Left in his chains too long, his wild and masculine spirit will die.

The famous Greek philosopher Epictetus once said, "No

man is free who is not the master of himself.". Along with Seneca, he referred to the practice of stoicism and man's mastery of his own impulses, desires, and emotions. This has led to the debate between men who have been taught that they should not express their feelings and the radical rainbow-haired feminist trolls that seek only the emasculation of men claiming that men are dangerous and volatile because their emotions aren't left unchecked.

There is a half-truth on both sides of the argument. Stay with me. This is not a defense of the rainbow-haired mongrels, but the practice of extreme stoicism is just as damaging to a man as becoming a giant useless blob of unchecked emotions. I cannot say whether or not the Greek stoics intended their words to be interpreted as they are today because, well, they're dead, and I can't ask them. But this black and white interpretation of stoicism has graced the pages of numerous self-help books and blogs that you can find literally everywhere.

"No man is free who is not the master of himself." sounds pretty awesome, but for a man to be the master of himself, he must be the master of all of his elements. He cannot ever be free so long as there is another master who holds the keys to his nature, including stoicism. The other extreme is also damaging because for a man to freely submit to his nature, he becomes more like his feminine counterparts, an endless sea of emotions and impulses. For a man to become his own master, he must achieve a balance between these two extremes.

A man must chain his emotions, but as the master of them, he must also be discerning and allow them to go free when necessary. A man should talk about his feelings, but not to every woman who has an elaborate delusion about *fixing him* as he is not broken, to begin with. To truly be that master of himself, a man cannot outsource the elements of himself to the empire that demands he submit to a more feminine way of life. Instead, he must reject the empire's notion that he must be controlled and locked behind a glass case until he is needed and disregard the feminist pleas that only seek to undermine his true nature.

Unlike the stoics Epictetus and Seneca, whose works were

heavily influenced by him, Plato's works seemed to better grasp man's true nature. He is noted to have believed that a man's soul was the sum of three distinctive parts represented by a chariot. The chariot in his example was made up of a white horse, a dark horse, and lastly, the rider that piloted them both.

The dark horse represented man's most base desires and appetites, his impulses and unpredictability. The white horse represented man's *thumos*. While there is no one word in the English language that can effectively describe it, *thumos* was referred to by the Greeks as the seat of life itself. It was the source of man's righteous anger and emotion, his spirit that balked at the notion of someone unwilling to live up to a determined code of honor.

It is the fire that resides within man that makes him a complete man. *Thumos is masculinity.* The rider represented the bridge between the white and the dark horse, which had the sole purpose of maintaining the balance between the opposing natures of the two wild beasts.

The empire has not only sought to disrupt the balance between the two mighty steeds but has sentenced the white horse to be put out to pasture, making the chariot that is a man's soul weaker and slower. Likened to a keystone being removed from a stone castle, the removal man's thumos reduces him to nothing more than a slave to his appetites. Left to run on its own, the dark horse will pull the chariot straight into oblivion.

It isn't difficult to draw a parallel between the chariot drawn only by the dark horse and the empire's preference for the modern man whose will is eroded into submission by today's hyper-consumerist culture. Televised sports, an endless stream of pornography at his fingertips, action movies, political outrage, and so on are all tools meant to pacify his thumos, his fire. By living vicariously through indirect conflict, he is tricked into believing that he is a man doing manly things. But his soul is not so easily deceived.

Even with these distractions of the mind, the man within the empire is plunged into a deep malaise. He can feel that something is missing, but he cannot quite articulate what it is. As the dark horse pulls him further into oblivion, the rider's uneasiness becomes evident as he shifts listlessly, longing for the primordial vigor of life that eludes him. He is like a junkie that developed a tolerance for his drug of choice and must consume more and more to keep the fire under control.

Unable to contain the blaze, the man will lash out violently and irrationally at anyone, everyone, even himself. A volcanic eruption of unfostered thumos and fire destroys everything in its path as it cascades down the side of his mountainous being until all that was locked inside is finally spent. Out of every 10 suicides, 7 of them were men, and 99.9% of all mass shootings are perpetrated by men who had reached their breaking point.

With no white horse to correct the course and keep his desires and appetite at bay, he was forced to go to war with himself and the world around him. With the realization that the odds were stacked against him in this war of attrition, he made the decision that if he could not win the battle, he would at least end it on his own terms.

Years of stifling my own thumos and trying to be a good citizen of the empire nearly led me straight off of the cliff some years ago. The feeling of being trapped within yourself is one that numerous men can relate to, and it has become the greatest epidemic this world has ever seen. It does not discriminate. It attacks the young, the old, the sick, and the healthy alike.

Without both horses pulling at the chariot, man is faced with a terrifying doom that could be avoided if he only stopped waiting for permission from the empire to be what he truly is and is always meant to be.

The structural integrity of a man is dependent on the presence of all of the elements of his soul. Each stone has a purpose and holds all of the others in their proper place. As the old saying goes, if it's moving, it's broken. The absence of just one of the stones will result in even the tallest and broadest of towers to crumble into dust.

This is why a man cannot remain within the empire without falling to the hands of a dark and wild beast that seeks only to run straight to its own demise. If he chooses to live life as he was meant to live it, he must breach the walls and escape the civilization in which he finds himself to find the civilization that resides *within* himself as T.K. Whipple described it.

Whipple stated that our ancestors possessed civilization within themselves as the wild existed in the external. The harsh and rugged conditions in which they lived enforced the need to develop certain psychological traits that enabled them to survive. Their everyday lives consisted of struggles and challenges that, without these traits, would have killed them rather quickly.

In the same way that you get your looks and physical traits passed down from your parents, these primal and primitive psychological traits that our ancestors developed over a millennium of evolution have been passed down to us as well. This is great for men, but it also creates a problem.

This modern empire in which we find ourselves has stripped all wildness from its landscape in its relentless march toward progress. The external need for these primal instincts and traits has all but vanished outside of a few third-world countries and Amazonian tribes. Man no longer needs these things to survive. These attributes made them men in the first place.

But these are a product of our evolution. This modern and civilized world that we live in is only a speck on the timeline of our entire collective existence. Throughout all known history, the need for man's thumos to combat the wild and untamed world has been present for far longer than not. For ages, the elements of man, the white horse, have been needed, and the expectation that it should just willingly be out to pasture is foolhardy at best.

This nature was bred into us out of necessity, and it cannot be turned off with some flick of a switch simply because the need was removed. This is what we are now, and we cannot devolve into lesser beings. We have no choice but to embrace our complete selves regardless of whether or not the empire is willing to allow us to.

Those within the empire tell us that the sun has set on

the age of men and that we are merely square pegs in a world made of round holes. This leaves us pacing within ourselves like beasts that have been stolen from the wilderness. They have built condos and fine dining establishments right there on the mountain and now expect the creature to wear clothes, sit upright, and accept that he is now obsolete.

We have been told to "evolve" because the age where men are needed has ended. This is nothing more than a polite way of saying we should become more like women if we wish to remain welcome here among the civilized rabble.

While going entirely off-the-grid and choosing to live as one's ancestors may be appealing and even possible to some, this isn't the case for everyone. A new balance must be struck where a man can be as he is intended, but the empire has shown no signs of allowing this to happen. Instead, we are expected to live half-lives and be pulled along by the dark horse while offering no resistance whatsoever.

This relatively new sedentary lifestyle that we are expected to embrace has left us anxious and pacing. It is intolerable, and unless we are resigned to allow our thumos to die as many already have, we must resist. This empire that seeks to quell the flames of man is the enemy that we have been longing to fight. It is the mountain that we have hungered to climb, and the only way to conquer it is to return to a way of living that feeds our soul.

But as stated earlier, we cannot go back to living as our ancestors once did, nor should we as it would dishonor them and spit on everything that they fought so hard to build. Instead, we must find our own balance that resists the empire's steady degrading march to effeminacy. Since we cannot go back, we must go forward but in a new direction and reclaim our own seat of life.

Population control seems to be on the agenda of the empire as more and more people rally behind the idea that husbands and wives should stop having children. NO. It is a man's duty to himself and his ancestors that he furthers his bloodline and creates a legacy. This is our chance for immortality.

In October of 2020, I was a speaker at the Patriarchs event

of the 21 Convention in Orlando, Florida. In my speech, I spoke of legacy and how a man's legacy was his path to true immortality. As a man, you are obligated to further your bloodline for the sake of your tribe's survival. As a father, your duty to your children is to foster them into both good men and women that are also good at being men and women.

When you die, your children will take possession of your belongings. Whatever they don't want will either be donated or thrown away. Their children, your grandchildren, will get whatever is left after a lifetime of things being misplaced or broken when your children die. By the time your great-grandchildren are born, there will likely be nothing physical left to pass down except for one thing.

Your legacy.

Being a father places you as the most influential figure in the lives of your children, or at the very least, it should. The empire may try to change that all they want, but it is incumbent upon you to not allow that to happen. By raising your children in a way that is honorable, they will, in turn, raise their children the same way. Your grandchildren, having been raised honorably, will then, in turn, raise their children in the same honorably and so forth and so on.

Your great-grandchildren and all of those who will come after may not remember your name or even know anything about you, but their character and desire to live honorable lives will have come from you. This is the true meaning of legacy. I am reminded of a line from the Russel Crowe movie, Gladiator. *"Hold the line! Stay with me! If you find yourself alone, riding in the green fields with the sun on your face, do not be troubled. For you are in Elysium [Heaven], and you're already dead!* **Brothers, what we do in life... echoes in eternity."**

"What we do in this life..."

Those words alone should be enough to reignite the fire in your belly. The empire is a world that was created for the dark horse. Not only will it try relentlessly to shame, shape, and mold you into a lesser being, your own echoes will be what shapes the lives of the men you are charged with leading. By fostering your own white horse, your thumos, your echoes will be well received by your children and grandchildren. The structural integrity of your tribe is all that stands between a legacy worth honoring and a life half lived by all those that will come after.

The seat of life itself that rests within the soul of man is an echo from his ancestors. The psychological traits that were passed down to us from our ancestors are that ancient calling, that primal roar that we can feel deep in our balls. What we do in this life can either further that echo, or it can drown it out. By choosing to further the legacy of those that came before us and establish our own, man must hold on to all of the pieces of himself as tightly as he can.

A man who maintains his structural integrity is a man that can withstand his intended load, the burdens of life, and the responsibilities that he is destined to take up in his quest to build a lasting legacy. He can place his feet firmly on the ground and never falter from fracture or fatigue. Yes, he will be tested. The dark horse will always bite and pull at the reigns in an attempt to run straight into doom, but it is his thumos that he worked to foster and strengthen that will overtake his darkness and hold the chariot to the path.

CHAPTER SEVEN
DETERMINATION

*Did you tackle that trouble that came your way, With a resolute heart
and cheerful? Or hide your face from the light of day, With a craven
soul and fearful? Oh, a trouble's a ton, or a trouble's an ounce, Or
a trouble is what you make it, And it isn't the fact that you're hurt
that counts, But only how did you take it? You are beaten to earth?
Well, well, what's that? Come up with a smiling face. It's nothing
against you to fall down flat, But to lie there -- that's disgrace. The
harder you're thrown, why the higher you bounce; Be proud of
your blackened eye! It isn't the fact that you're licked that counts,
It's how did you fight -- and why? And though you be done to the
death, what then? If you battled the best you could, If you played
your part in the world of men, Why, the Critic will call it good.
Death comes with a crawl, or comes with a pounce, And whether
he's slow or spry, It isn't the fact that you're dead that counts,*

But only how did you die?

- Edmund Vance Cooke; How did you die?

"How did you die?"

It isn't uncommon for many men to romanticize their own
deaths. The thought of *going out in a blaze of glory* has entered my
own mind many times. But the chances of that actually happening are very slim given the relatively mundane nature of society
today. Still, the thought of standing before a great army and fighting until your last breath stokes the fire in a man's heart like nothing else.

In Cooke's poem, How did you die?; it's ironic that the only
mention of death is in the last two lines while the majority spoke
of life and how it was lived. Was it lived in fear? Did you pull back
from the face of danger or adversity? Or did you live your life with
purpose and grit?

There is an old saying that death is easy, but living is what's actually hard. It takes courage, strength, honor, and structural integrity to possess grit and determination. Without these elements, a man is doomed to merely exist. It is living that is the proper function of a man. He is not to wile away his days, seeking to prolong them by avoiding all of the things that would challenge him.

No, his purpose is to dare to greatness while acknowledging his own mortality.

Again, death is easy, and everyone can do it without effort. But for a man to truly live, he must accept his inborn proclivities for risk and danger and seek out a path of honor and glory.

I envy the brave men that were afforded the opportunity to answer the call to greatness during World War Two. They were given a chance that the generation of men today was not. There have indeed been wars and conflicts throughout the modern age, but nothing on such a scale as the second world war. It was a war between mighty empires that took the blood of more men than almost any other conflict to date to fight and win it.

I keep returning to this point because it is crucial that you, the reader, understand that you should not have a longing for a life lived in a different time or that this time we have been given should regress to that of the centuries or decades past. We were simply born too late to explore the world and much too soon to explore the far reaches of the universe. And because of this, the conflicts that were and will be attributed to those times will never fall within our grasp. Therefore we must toil and search deeper within ourselves for ways to satisfy our hunger for greatness.

The empire sees this hunger as problematic, to say the least. Starting with young boys, these behaviors such as aggression and risk-taking are viewed as something that is toxic and must be squashed or somehow bred out of them. It feels that boys must be deprogrammed at a young age to create a more ideal and more effeminate version of a man that is more manageable.

In the early to mid-1990s, we saw a substantial increase in the amount of ADHD cases, predominantly in young and teenage boys who were berated and beaten into submission by a flood of medications designed to make them sit down, be still, and shut up. All of the things that men were not created to do.

The inherent nature of young boys is to be drawn to chaos so that they can impose their will upon it in an effort to create order. Where there is no chaos, they will create it. This is why boys will typically struggle more to assimilate into a classroom setting than girls. They are not meant or designed to be pliable. This need to impose their will on the world around them is something that must be fostered rather than quelled.

This unyielding determination isn't something that has to be chosen by men and young boys; it is hardwired into their brains. Yet as is seen time and time again, the empire wishes to hold the trademark rights on will and power. Any man who seeks to impose his own upon the world around him is slapped with a cease and desist order, courtesy of the elites.

Why shouldn't we just simply allow ourselves and our young boys to be reshaped to fit the bill of the empire's expectations? If we snuffed out the determination bred into us to conquer and create order from chaos and just go-with-the-flow, would that make for an easier life? The truth is that, yes, it would. But that kind of life would effectively kill us all, men and women, alike.

The empire likes to forget that it was built on struggle and on the imposing of man's will on a world full of chaos to bring it to order. This is man's destiny. This is what he was created to do. The determination to fight back against forces beyond his control is the oxygen that feeds his thumos. Take that away, and his very soul will begin to atrophy.

Take a look back to the 1960s when NASA was first putting men into space. They had hypothesized that the effects of a zero-gravity environment would have a positive impact on the astronauts. They reasoned that without the pressure of earth's gravity pulling them down, even more growth and health would be made possible. As it turns out, they couldn't have been more wrong. Without gravity and pressure, the astronauts start to experience atrophy in both their musculature and their organs.

Now apply this same principle to life. Without the presence of pressure from an outside force, a man in all of his being will start to atrophy. There is not one single trait possessed by a man that was not developed out of necessity. Nature doesn't create out of excess; it creates out of the need for survival.

The empire is only looking at the surface layer when it claims to have created a world where the need for survival is no longer required but provided to a man on a silk pillow of convenience. Why should a man fight when he doesn't have to? This question is loaded because the fact is that man needs to fight now more than ever, but without the presence of an external force, the forces inside of himself are where he must take this fight.

Rather than fight to survive within the world, man must fight to achieve self-actualization. That may sound a little "woo woo," but it could not be further from the truth.

There are two definitions of the word determination. The first is the firmness of purpose or a sense of resoluteness. Man's only purpose in life is to create order. He holds power over the world, a power that was given to him by the gods. He creates the world around him by naming it. This act of creation is almost divine, and to deny it is to remove the need for his very existence. The second definition of determination and perhaps the most important when discussing a man's actualization is the process of establishing something exactly through calculated measure.

The self-actualization of man is achieved through the calculated measure of will imposed. Without it, he is never fully aware of what he is. By refusing to walk a path of resistance and resigning himself to be swept along by the current, he effectively abandons his own determination. He denies himself knowing and experiencing what he truly is.

But that is the crux. The empire, in all its wisdom, has determined that there is no longer a need for an actualized man. The culture of the empire is now centered around being provided for rather than the encouragement to provide for oneself. You see this amongst your peers anytime you set your mind to something meant to make you better or stronger.

This goes back to the crabs-in-a-bucket. Any attempt to climb out of the bucket is met with resistance by those that wish only to stay within the safety and security that has been provided for them. A look deeper will show that this isn't out of their own need to climb out before you, but rather a need to preserve their own safety and security. This behavior suggests that there are different classes of men—those that need to be ruled and those that simply cannot be ruled by anyone.

The act of becoming something more in their eyes is seen as an attack on them, and in response, they will fight to retain their own equilibrium and understanding of the world around them. To them, vertical honor must only be given to the elite class that provides for them, and they will stop at almost nothing to prevent their peers from migrating to another class. But this resistance is actually a blessing to the man fighting to free himself from the bucket; it is the resistance, the chaos, that he needs to thrive.

In his book, Wild at Heart, contemporary Christian Author John Eldredge stated that "Deep in his heart, every man longs for a battle to fight, an adventure to live, and a beauty to rescue.", this battle between man and empire, between subjugation and sovereignty, is but the first step in the self-actualization of a man. The determination of his being.

The battle, the adventure to live, and the beauty to rescue all make up the crucible in which a man is truly made. You can call it a rite of passage of sorts that must take place in order for the transition from boy to man to take place—a demarcation line between two worlds. No man is capable of real actualization without first passing through some sort of crucible. As we know, the current state of the empire has all but removed every opportunity for this to occur.

The lack of an existing right of passage is really at the fault of the development of western culture. Prior to grand-scale gentrification, most cultures understood the need to separate a young boy from feminine influence once he reached a certain age. In many cases, this was the mother and was more than just a symbolic act. It was necessary to his biological and psychological development that the boy be heavily influenced by other men during those years where he was most susceptible to influence.

The men and elders of a tribe would storm into the home as the mother (who knew the importance of this and was in on it) would scream and plead as her young son was removed from the house by force and taken far away from his village into the wild to live among the men of his tribe where they would mold him into one of them.

It was there that he would undergo his crucible. He would be taught the skills needed to survive and then, through the act of ritual, would either be left to fend for himself for a predetermined amount of time or forced to complete a task that was assigned to only the men of the tribe. Through this process, he would be taught by both the wisdom of his captors and his own personal journey what he was truly made of.

Today there is no such tradition that exists in the western world because the culture no longer supports the need for it. The assimilation of multiple tribes into the grand empire that has taken on the role of ancient men for itself watered down these traditions. It replaced them with something more universally accepted. Outside of extreme circumstances, the likelihood of a boy or young man passing through a crucible, at least one described as a rite of passage, is very low.

Instead, there is the epidemic of extended adolescence. There are no longer events outside of the random that are intended to help bring a boy across the threshold into manhood. Rites of passage are now reduced to high school graduations, earning a driver's license, or becoming a husband and father. Even modern education has now been reduced to only providing general knowledge without imparting any real experience or wisdom needed to navigate life in the contemporary world. The process of determination of a man has been lost.

Since the empire has removed the need for these rites, men and fathers must work outside the walls to create their own within their families. Even at the scale of the community, there is minimal alignment in beliefs and values unless a deliberate effort is made to create a community of those that do share the same values. The Mormon communities in Utah are an excellent example of this.

But how can we go about creating these new rites of passage to save our boys from the tragedy that is never truly becoming men? It really isn't feasible to have you and your buddies from work burst through the door while your son is sitting at the table eating his chicken tenders and carry him off into the night as your wife screams for her baby boy. Just imagine what child protective services and the police would have to say about that when they answer the call from your poor horrified neighbors.

Still, the need for a young boy to pass through these rites and return as a man are imperative if there is to be any hope in the fight for his soul. Like most of us, we missed out on the opportunity for this, and either had to try to figure it out on our own or, in many cases, are still lost trying to figure out what it is to be a man

It isn't hard to see that the latter is the case for most men in society today. Especially when you consider the sheer number of fatherless homes where young boys are taught what it means to be a man by tv screens, celebrities, and women only to later discover that the world isn't as they were told. This epidemic has been the undoing of men and has further led to the degradation of masculine men in western culture.

The solution, however, is a simple one. Fathers and men who are in the lives of the young men in their families must take up the ancient role of the tribal men and create new rites of passage. They must act to preserve and foster the fiery thumos that await discovery within the young men's hearts.

When creating your own rites of passage, it is vital that they consist of three clear and distinctive phases. The first phase must always be separation. Similar to the tribesmen tearing a young boy from his mother's arms, fathers must work with their sons to separate them from their current childish self and feminine influence. This can be done by the forced shedding of childish possessions like security blankets and practices such as always running to their mother whenever something is difficult or scary. It must symbolize that a particular part of his life has ended and must be discarded in order to make room for new growth into the next.

The second is the transition phase. In a tribal culture, the boy would have been between worlds at this point. He is no longer a boy, but his determination as a man would not yet be complete, leaving him in him a blank slate, a cocoon awaiting metamorphosis. During this phase, he would be taught the knowledge, skills, and duties required of him to live as a man within the tribe. Things such as hunting to provide food or training to become a warrior were restricted to only the men of the tribe.

Within the modern home, this transition phase can be awkward for both the father and the son. Fathers who do not have clearly defined roles within their household cannot effectively teach their son what is necessary for him to begin his journey toward fulfilling that role himself. Yes, in this instance, I am referring to gender roles.

Regardless of how frowned upon it is to the empire, without the assignment of clearly defined gender roles that separate the men of the tribe from the women, this transition from boy to man cannot occur as the lines are blurred.

These roles are personal and unique to each family, of course, but there needs to be a separation between the masculine and the feminine. One example of this separation is that the men are expected to perform any duty that involves risk or intense physical labor in my own family. Once my boys reached a certain age, they were taken out and taught to use firearms, chop wood for our winter stores, and maintain the yard.

I taught them skills such as carpentry and plumbing, basic automobile maintenance, and we also began physical training with weights to ensure that they became strong.

Outside of this, they were taught how they were expected to conduct themselves as young men as far as behavior and the acceptance of personal responsibility. No longer were they allowed to rely on myself or their mother for menial tasks that they were capable of doing themselves.

If they wanted a car or anything outside of their basic survival needs, it was their responsibility to earn money for it. I taught them that they were expected to resolve their own conflicts with outsiders and even let them fail and face the consequences of their failures while showing them the way forward from those failures.

The idea is to let them fail so that they understand the cause and effect of their efforts or lack thereof. While still being in a controlled environment, I can step in should things get out of hand, but for the most part, I am nothing more than the guardrail that separates them from the edge. If I want them to be able to navigate life as a man, I have to be willing to let them scrape some paint off the side should they veer too far from the road while ensuring that they don't drive completely over the cliffside.

The transition phase is meant to be painful and uncomfortable. It is intended to be a crucible, a gauntlet that is to be run and completed by the young boy. It should test both his will as well as your own. You will feel the pressure to lighten up or cut him some slack because seeing your boy growing into a man is painful.

The loss of their innocence is a milestone that parents aren't keen on witnessing in their children, but the fact remains that the empire will show no mercy to the boy. It will eat him alive if he does not possess the skills necessary to withstand the slow erosion of himself into the swath of a purposeless existence.

The final phase of these rites is the reintegration of the then boy, now *man*, into the tribe and his first steps into his new role. Tribal societies and cultures would celebrate the boys' return with a community feast to welcome the newly minted man. This aspect of the final phase was perhaps the most important as it was critical that the tribe now recognized him as a man and continued to regard him as such.

His mother would have to refrain from her natural instinct to smother and nurture him, recognizing that he was no longer her little boy that needed to be taken care of. The men and elders of the tribe would now recognize him as one of their own and help guide him on his journey as he was now allowed to take part in tasks and events reserved for only the men of the tribe. He was expected to pull his own weight and contribute to the tribe as a valuable member.

A modern family unit must treat their son no different. The temptation to allow him to revert back to his boyish ways must be resisted at all costs if the boy is to be able to accept his new role and status within the family. This will be particularly difficult for his mother. There is a special bond between a mother and her son that cannot be replicated and unique to the pair, just like a bond between fathers and sons cannot be replicated elsewhere.

As the father, the tribal leader, your role is to ensure that everyone in the family now recognizes him as a man. He may not yet be a legal adult, but his responsibilities are now that of a man's. His actions and the way that he is regarded within the family must indicate that he is determined or classified as a man, a young man who is still considered a junior member of the tribe, but a man nonetheless.

This act of taking your sons through a rite of passage is only possible if you yourself have crossed the rubicon into manhood. You cannot raise and foster a man if you have not fully embraced your role as a man, and your actions and conduct must reflect that. But there is yet another task that you yourself must have completed.

You must first pass through your own rite of passage. At 33 years old, I had thought that the hardships and struggles that I had endured and overcome had placed me above that of my peers. Having become a father at a young age and worked every day since to provide for my family. I had fallen victim to the illusion that I was doing everything required of me to be regarded as a man.

I followed the rules, I provided for my family, and I paid my taxes on time, but I still never felt as if I was complete. It wasn't until last summer that I was forced to be brutally honest with myself and discover who I was. To do that, I needed to be alone. I decided to go on a solo camping trip as far away from anyone else as possible and take some time to completely isolate myself from the world.

set off to the Appalachian Mountains in western North Carolina to a trail that I had hiked before with my sons a year prior. My aim was to cut from the trail and trek deep into the woods in search of a place where I could spend a few days alone. I had never done anything like it before and needed to know if I could. Having been in the area before, I was well aware that once up there, I would be disconnected from everyone as there was no cell phone service at the head of the trail, much less once I got further along.

I had taken only a small ax, a knife, a few gallons of water, and a couple pounds of elk jerky to survive on and knew right from the beginning that this would be difficult. In my hubris, I saw myself succeeding without too much of a struggle like most men today often imagine themselves doing. I pulled into the ranger station and made one final call to my wife and children before heading down the trail with my hand-drawn map that I had made from the satellite images I downloaded to my phone.

After the first two miles down the trail, I found the spot where I was to cross the Horsepasture River and made my way to the other side. That was it. I was officially alone. There were no trails on that side of the river, nor was it possible to cross without swimming for several miles. I continued to follow the river for roughly five more miles before coming to a bend where I was supposed to turn north and continue on for about an hour to a waterfall where I had seen a small clearing. That was where I was to make my camp.

My shoulders and legs ached from the weight of my pack, and in my head, I knew that this was the smallest challenge that I would face on this trip. I summoned up all of the grit I could and powered through until I finally reached my destination. Once I arrived, I unrolled my tarp and started setting up my tent. Checking my watch, it was about 9am, and the sky looked as if it was getting ready to open, so I gathered as much dry wood as I could and brought it inside my tent so that I would be able to build a fire later that night.

Now a man's thoughts can be his own worst enemy when he is without distraction. There's nothing to reign them in other than trying to find something to keep him busy. As I sat there in my tent listening to the rain pelting my tent, my mind began to wander. I thought of all of the mistakes I had made in my marriage and also with my kids. There had been quite a few. There had been numerous reports of black bear sightings all over the area, and I wondered, if I were to not make it home for any reason, how my wife and children would remember me.

Time is cruel when you're all alone. It seems to pass much slower without someone to turn and talk to. The temperature had dropped with the rain, and as I sat trying to warm myself, my thoughts continued to berate me. The silence deep within those mountains was deafening, and even the roar of the waterfall acted only as white noise and did very little to distract me.

If you've ever been alone with your own thoughts for an extended period of time, then you know what it feels like to feel trapped within your own head. Miles away from the nearest other people in the wide-open Appalachian wilderness, I still felt as if I were locked in a cage. It couldn't have been later than eight in the evening when I decided that I would go to sleep to try to make it through to the next morning and pass the grueling hours.

But sleep didn't come easy. As I lay there in the tent with my mind still racing, I was miserable. This was harder than I thought it would be because I hadn't considered the psychological strain of being truly alone. Looking back now, I see that this was my separation phase. I didn't strike out with the intention of this being a rite of passage by any means, but it truly was.

I was separated from all of the things and people that I had been using to identify who I was as a man. As I lay there in my tent with the hour-long seconds ticking by, I realized that I couldn't say who I was. For years I had been using my wife and children as markers for my identity. I had no North Star outside of my role as a husband and a father. No mission or purpose that was independent of my family. What was it that made me, me? What was it that made me a man? Who was I?

My transition phase came the next morning as I had the entire day to pass completely alone. I made my fire, had some jerky and water for breakfast, and went exploring a bit. Time passed a little quicker, and I still felt trapped in my own head, but I managed to get some things settled. Being alone and wholly separated from all of the distractions had allowed me some room to grow.

It's an odd thing to not hear one's own voice for a couple of days. I completely understand now why Tom Hanks had Wilson. But in those hours out there alone, I came to discover things about myself that I didn't know were there. I cannot accurately describe it, but something happened. I saw both myself and the rest of the world differently than I had before.

That night was the last night I spent out there, not because I had some profound epiphany, but rather because a storm system had moved in, and the heavy rains were causing the river to rise and become uncrossable. At around three in the morning, I was jolted from sleep when somehow water started getting into my tent, so I made the decision to pack everything up and leave during the next lull.

After getting all of my gear secured, I dumped the remainder of my water and food save for enough to get me back to the trail.

With nothing but a flashlight in hand and a small lantern clipped to the straps on my pack, I fought my way through the small mudslide that cascaded down the ridge.

The rain was coming down in buckets. It was pitch black, and there was no beaten path that I could follow, so I had to make an educated guess about the direction I was taking. I finally came to the bend in the river and followed it all the way back to my original crossing point. Thankfully, the giant boulders weren't yet completely submerged, and I could use them to get back across.

After making it across the river, I was finally back on the trail that I could follow all the way back. I was soaked, exhausted, and my legs were on fire, but I knew that this would be my final test. There was no reason why I couldn't stop and rest, but I wouldn't let myself. I had to keep going until I made it to my car. When I finally made it back, I was utterly wiped out. I threw my soaking wet pack in the back and climbed into the seat.

All I wanted was to get home and see my family. Still, I decided not to call them and chose to make the two-and-a-half-hour drive back time enough for me to reorganize my thoughts. I knew that when I arrived home, I would have to start living a more intentional life. It wasn't enough for me to just go with the flow anymore.

I needed not to expect my wife and children to see me any differently than they did just a few days before, and it will be important that you do the same when you reintegrate back into the world from your own rites. The changes and new discoveries that I had made were my own. They were internal, and the only way my family would see them would be through my actions and a new behavior model.

A rite of passage is simply a journey through a doorway. Once you get to the other side, there is an entirely different room that you still have to live in. The code of conduct and responsibilities are different, and just because you made it there doesn't mean that the work is done. In fact, it's just beginning.

As you create rites for your own sons to pass through, you must make this clear. Becoming a man is only the first step of the journey. They must now lead their lives as men with you there to guide them. There will eventually come a time when they will strike out on their own to start their own branch of the tribe, and the same temptations of the empire will still be there. Whether or not they can resist them is entirely upon how well you have prepared them.

Like you, they will falter and stumble from time to time, but the ability to draw from the lessons and guidance you have given them will make all the difference. It's when they are finally faced with the test of their own manhood will the determination finally be made.

CHAPTER EIGHT
DISCIPLINE

*"The one quality which sets one man apart from another,
the key which lifts one to every aspiration, while others are
caught up in the mire of mediocrity – is not talent, formal
education, nor intellectual brightness. It is self-discipline.
With self-discipline all things are possible. Without it, even
the simplest goal can seem like the impossible dream."*
-Teddy Roosevelt

It's a safe bet to say that any form of self-imposed discipline is a rarity in most people within the empire. We live in a culture of excess and gluttony. We live in a time of leisure and the acceptance of overindulgence just because something *feels good.* There's no need to refrain from going too far with anything anymore regardless of the consequences because it's either expected to be accepted by everyone or, at the very least, there's a pill for it.

As it turns out, ol' Teddy was right. Being disciplined indeed does set one man apart from another. It flies in the face of the current culture that everyone must be mediocre while only the ones who enforce such mediocrity are to be elevated in an effort to keep everyone equal. But men are meant to be free, and to be free means that equality isn't possible. Someone will always be better in some way, and if one is to rise, he must set himself apart from the rest.

A quote often attributed to Alexander the Great says, *"When Alexander saw the breadth of his domain, he wept for there were no more worlds to conquer."* that was pulled, and actually misquoted, from the works of Plutarch. You may even remember the quote from the movie Die Hard where Hans Gruber mentioned it a few moments before he shot Mr. Takagi in the head.

While the quote isn't historically accurate, mainly due to a terrible translation, it does, however, bring about a good point. Alexander the Great was perhaps one of the most accomplished conquerors ever to walk the earth. By the time he was just 21 years old, he had laid claim to most of the known world. Needless to say, his power and influence were well known to almost everyone.

But there was yet one world that can be argued that he could not conquer if the misquote was to be taken as historical fact. Of all of the things that he conquered, it implies a lack of power and control of the world within himself. *He wept because there were no more worlds to conquer.* One could assume that he sought to conquer everything because, as a man, that is what he was bred to do. However, there are many instincts and tendencies that we as men must reign in from time to time, and it would seem that the need to conquer was something that Alexander did not have control over.

For a man to conquer himself, he must first understand himself. For thousands of years, man feared the strike of lightning and the roar of thunder before he developed an understanding of what they actually were. It was only when he gained this understanding of lightning and electricity itself that man could become the master of the thing that he once could not control. Man's desire and appetites, his dark horse pulling the chariot, is no different.

The only way for a man to become the master of himself is through self-discipline. Each day of his existence, a man is either a king or a slave to his humanness. Saying simply, *I am what I am,* is a surrender to another master and the forfeiture of one's own crown. A man is not made great for what he is but through what he becomes each and every day.

The surrender to himself and his dark horse makes him a victim of external circumstance that rules over him. He is like Alexander, who had conquered everything else while still failing to defeat Alexander. He was a slave to his own passions, and being unable to bring them under his control was beset by an unfulfilled life.

The modern world, the empire, and its culture have made it more convenient than ever to succumb to human weakness while using the same slave-like justification of, "I am what I am.". Here in the widely interconnected world, distractions are everywhere, and the temptation to indulge in them is even greater. How long can you go after waking without looking at your smartphone or social media?

How difficult is it to rise out of bed early in the morning to go workout in the gym? What about the lies and justifications that you make to yourself when trying to halt an addiction? You're just like everyone else and will remain so without becoming disciplined and conquering that tumultuous world within yourself.

Going back to what Teddy Roosevelt had said in his quote, self-discipline is the one thing that sets a man apart from another, but it is also what sets a man apart from himself and his self-imposed chains. It is what makes all of his aspirations possible, while those that he has differentiated himself from are left behind on the muddy lands of mediocrity. Was Alexander truly a conqueror? He had conquered the world, but his own passions left him longing for more to conquer. If he wished to conquer everything he laid his eyes upon, then in his own mind, he hadn't conquered everything yet. He was still a slave to the man in his own reflection.

A man in today's world is a slave to both temptation as well as himself. Each day he is presented with an opportunity to conquer himself over and over again, but the empire longs to keep him pacified and content. The cheap dopamine hits that trick him into false contentment only last so long, so he must continue to indulge in his search for superficial satisfaction. This is a never-ending struggle.

A slave will never be truly content with being a slave even if he is granted a temporary respite from the whip but must become completely free and gain power over his own life. As men, we must rule over ourselves. We must gain some power of our own and exercise that power. For a man to gain power over himself, he is to first understand his weaknesses.

Alexander failed to realize that he was subservient to his

passions, and today's most modern men are very much the same. Slaves to comfort and convenience because there really is no need to be otherwise in order to survive. But again, a man's life is not merely about survival but more about actually living. A life of just existing is not enough for him.

The empire made men slaves to comfort by providing it so freely. The self-mastery and power of oneself can only come from actively seeking discomfort simply for the sake of it. Rejecting the temptation of immediate comfort in exchange for temporary pain sounds unnatural, but it could not be more natural or more necessary. The natural resistance to any kind of discipline, self-imposed or otherwise, is derived from our early years when we prided ourselves as rebels without a cause.

As a father of teenagers, it's easy now to look at them and myself at that age. There was actually no reason for me to rebel against anything, even though my home life was far from perfect. But still, I rationalized my decisions as simply the consequences of growing up without a father. He had died before I even started school, and the influence of other men was all but absent. While that may have had a lot to with my behavior, it wasn't the sole cause of it.

Being a rebel without a cause just sounds sexy. The illusion of absolute freedom that it offers seduces man into thinking that he is living on the fringes of society and at odds with the world when he's just a useful idiot to the empire. The refusal to adhere to any rules or any particular path feeds into the allure of being a lone wolf when in reality, a man must have a cause to rebel against if he wants to be more than an angry teenager for his entire life.

Humans are very much like primates in that they share the natural instinct to rebel against any and all perceived authority. In both groups, most individuals are happy to go along for the ride as long as they aren't getting the short end of the stick. This works rather well in a scarcity-culture where resources are limited, and everyone must do their part to survive. There, everyone knows their place within the established hierarchy as well as the duty to their roles.

It's within a post-scarcity culture where resources are abundant, and it's much less of a risk to go in one's own direction that we see the rise of rebellion. You can take, for example, the United States both during WWII and afterward. During the years that the war raged on, resources were scarce, and many of them were rationed in a way that allowed for ample supplies to make it to the troops who were doing all the fighting.

The people back home in the states knew that resources were scarce and, for the majority, accepted their lot and did their part to contribute to the greater good. But this scarcity culture quickly vanished as the war came to an end and life returned to normal. There was an industrial boom during the war, and now resources were not as scarce as they were before, but there was one factor that is often unaccounted for.

The people who were at the bottom of the societal hierarchy during the war resented the fact that they were, well, at the bottom of the scale. They had done their part during the war due to the scarcity of resources, but that didn't mean that they were happy to just forget that they were looked over and often passed up for any opportunity to advance their station. There was a resentment that lingered, and now that resources were easy to obtain, a rebellion against the establishment began.

The hippies, as well as the *greasers* and the *beatniks*, all now sought a new path to a status that came from the level of contempt that they could receive from those that still held power. Because they knew they had gotten the short end of the stick when times were tough, they now acted like the beta chimps who had been abused by their alpha troop leader and sought to usurp the throne and install someone else in their place.

This need for rebellion exists today in the empire's resource-abundant culture. The cultural race to the bottom is a rebellion against the standards imposed by the baby boomers who had failed to see what was coming. They had rebelled against the previous generation and what it had done to them and failed to ever evolve from that point. Their own free-spiritedness and individualist nature cut like a double-edged sword. They don't even realize at this point that the rebels won and that they are now violently beating a corpse, trying to *kill it harder.*

In reality, there has never been a period of scarcity culture since WWII as resources and information have grown in abundance exponentially since then. Like the extension of adolescence that has been brought on by eliminating a need for rites of passage, the extension of rebellion has existed because of the lack of resource scarcity. Ironically, when everyone is rebelling, no one is. They have conformed without even realizing it.

There is, however, a new scarcity-culture that has arisen almost everywhere, but it is not as easily noticed as a scarcity of resources that are needed to survive. This era of conformity disguised as rebellion has hidden the fact that standards and accountability have now become the things in short supply. The citizens of the empire have spent so much time rebelling against everything that the culture of the empire has shifted. The original rebels have become the new leaders of the hierarchy, and they don't even realize it.

Like that one movie says, you either die a hero, or you live long enough to see yourself become the villain. These so-called rebels have created a pluralistic society where there is no competition for status between others within the empire. Status is now yet another resource that has become unlimited in its abundance when before gaining status in one arena or another, one had to compete with his peers and possess the discipline required to rise within the ranks.

This precisely what they wanted, but they are still pulled by the need to engage in some mythological fight against *the man.* This can only be explained by realizing an inherent need that lies within man to resist being controlled by some established power structure. Man needs an enemy, after all.

The need of an enemy to fight against can now be met without having to engage in the social dilemma that no longer exists. Before, if a man wanted to rise in status, someone else would have to come down as there was limited room on the ladder, and not everyone could make it all at once. Someone had to be a loser in order to find a winner. Now, this still exists, but on an entirely different scale than when the empire had peaked toward the end of WWII.

The pluralistic nature of the empire today brought about the introduction of participation trophies where everyone's a winner, and there are no losers all because little Timmy with the gimp felt bad that he couldn't beat big bad Johnny in the footrace. The same can be seen with the paths to success and status. But what is now being overlooked is that success is entirely relative and subjective to the individual.

Everyone is now so goddamned unique that they, by default, are successful in whatever the hell it is they do, and they demand that they be recognized and applauded for it. There is the illusion that there is no need for competition to achieve status because all status' matter. This new pluralistic culture's side effect is that now mediocrity is praised even though it grates against the nature of man.

Just look at the ridiculous notions that come with the latest idea that there are multiple genders that one can choose from. That Man and Masculinity alike have been redefined. Across numerous cultures, being determined to be a man is more than just a biological construct and a symbol of one's status within a tribe. You become a man from learning and performing the disciplines required of a man, but there the prerequisite for earning the status of man is that you had to be born a male.

Instead, the citizens of the empire have thrust themselves upon the altar of inclusivity and decided that being a man is simply a matter of choosing to be one. But quite frankly, I can call myself an astronaut if I want to, but if I've never gone up into space, it isn't anything more than a fantasy. If I wish to be an astronaut, then I must set myself apart. If one wishes to be a man, he must set himself apart from the empire that collectively decides that everyone is the same.

Without status to compete for among the masses, without resources to gain, or an enemy to fight, a man's determination must come from his tribe and from within himself. The siren's call to mediocrity must become his new enemy. His own weakness and the weakness of others must be looked at with disgust and pity. He must hate the possibility of a fate less than exceptional. This hate is the fuel that will drive him to develop the discipline needed to achieve his status as a man.

The definition of what it is to be a man means nothing to the empire and its citizens. To be a man is to be good at being a man, and being good at being a man is destructive and toxic to the empire. It comes with pain and ostracization from those around you that wish to receive praise for their mediocrity.

Self-discipline is the welcoming of pain over pleasure in exchange for a reward that is greater but not immediately seen or gained. The denial of one's own instant gratification sets him apart from the consumerist masses accepting their participation trophies with a sense of entitlement. The disciplined man knows that *he isn't,* therefore he must *become*, and the only path to becoming is through the ritual sacrifice of his own immediate comfort and gratification.

The disciplined man is loathed by those outside of his tribe because they are reminded of their own mediocrity. He exhibits his strength and power with an air of earned arrogance that refuses to allow him to afford praise to those who have achieved nothing. Those that have earned nothing condemn the disciplined man for this arrogance and even more so for the fact that this arrogance has merit within his own tribe. Others that have chosen to run the gauntlet even though they could have chosen not to give honor and respect to the disciplined man.

The tribe of disciplined men sets itself apart from the mediocre and chooses only to afford honor and respect to one another and denies the new pluralistic culture's merit. This culture of being entitled to equal praise for being less than equal is not welcome within the tribe of men who have embraced their true nature. They earned their place among their peers with their actions that answered the question that rests on every man's heart. *Am I enough*? They have paid the price of admission in full and offer no esteem to those who come up short. They accepted that they must become rather than just *be*, and so must everyone else. However, this isn't to say that they want everyone to be able to join the tribe, just the opposite, in fact. Should everyone rise to the tribal standards, those same standards would have to be raised to separate the wheat from the chaff to keep the tribe from growing more extensive than can be maintained effectively.

There must always be an us and them hierarchy within the realm of tribal men.

George Orwell's position on civilized versus uncivilized men expressed a polarity that implied an us and them hierarchy. Orwell argued that "Men can only be highly civilized while other men, inevitably less civilized, are there to guard and feed them.". So as being a man is a discipline developed through the constant practice of becoming good at being a man, the same can be said for the disciplined man. For the disciplined man to exist, there must, of course, be the undisciplined.

For the disciplined man to set himself apart from the undisciplined, he has no other choice than to align himself to an "us." This better illustrates the analogy drawn by Roosevelt. Like the baby boomer generation, their rebellion went mainstream. It became the *new normal,* a term that recently became popular during 2020 when the media fully embraced their role as fear monger and state-sponsored propagandists.

The rebellion against *the man* has become the new normal over the last several decades, and the pendulum has begun to swing the other way. Those that now choose to live more traditional and conservative lifestyles, or *TradCon,* are the new rebels but have been misidentified as the mythological and monolithic *man.* The irony of *#resist* being blasted all over social media by the hyper-woke social justice warriors validates the claim that they still see themselves as embroiled in a battle against an oppressive system that seeks to control them. They're so blinded by this notion that they fail to see that they have become the oppressors.

Men who practice being disciplined or being good at being men are now the outliers. They are the ones locked in battle with the depraved and oppressive system that seeks total control. One could argue that there should be a *live and let live* approach to this, but what sounds good on paper doesn't necessarily always work when put into practice. Both sides of the spectrum are conflict-driven and will inevitably seek to force their ideologies onto the other through whatever means available to them.

This declaration of war is one that was chosen both willingly and subconsciously as the innate desire for conflict still lies heavily in the hearts of all men regardless of which side of the wall they reside on. The only difference between the two is that the disciplined man knows what he is asking for and accepts it.

Becoming a disciplined man is a choice; it's proactive. It has to be with the abundance of luxuries and resources that are readily available in the 21st century. Without a full-on economic and societal collapse that seems to be a primarily held masturbatory fantasy by many, there is no real requirement for men to answer the ancient call to his nature other than because he simply chooses to.

Man must choose between being swept along with the tide and swimming against the wave of the modern and pluralistic culture that offers no visible path to honor and self-actualization. He must choose to become the new rebel, the antithesis of the empire, and the unwelcome barbarian.

Why make a choice to live life as a man when you'll likely receive no honor or accolades for it? Being disciplined at being a man is a way to be hated and discarded by a culture that outright refuses to appreciate the effort. But the point of it all isn't to get recognition or pats on the back. Even if they don't realize it, the disciplined man is a benefit to the empire. He is the keystone on which sustainable communities are built. It only looks like they are no longer needed on the surface. That is until they are.

While it may seem foolish or pointless to be prepared for a contingency that may never come, the cost of not could potentially be too great for all parties involved. Even if the day where he is called upon never dawns, the disciplined man can take satisfaction and pride in knowing that he was prepared nonetheless.

His preparedness enabled him to benefit his tribe as the capable sentry peering into the darkness with the campfire to his back as he searched for threats to those he protected.

He is set apart as a member of an honor group, men who have chosen the hard way over a life of ease. His hunger for a challenge is satisfied by his willingness to do battle with his own nature. He becomes the embodiment of the white horse, thumos itself, and carries that fire forward, lighting the way for other men to find their own torches to be lit.

CHAPTER NINE
SIMPLICITY

"No character can be simple unless it is based on truth—unless it is lived in harmony with one's own conscience and ideals. Simplicity is the pure white light of a life lived from within. It is destroyed by any attempt to live in harmony with public opinion. Public opinion is a conscience owned by a syndicate,—where the individual is merely a stockholder. But the individual has a conscience of which he is sole proprietor. Adjusting his life to his own ideals is the royal road to simplicity. Affectation is the confession of inferiority; it is an unnecessary proclamation that one is not living the life he pretends to live."
-    William George Jordan; Self Control, Its Kingship and Majesty

　　Developing a contempt for the things in life that are not essential to his being is the final stage of a man's decision to journey beyond the pale and forsake the walls of the empire. The rejection of its corruption is but the first. When a man sees everything that conflicts with his own nature as unnecessary noise, he has finally and truly shed his chains.

　　Nature abides by simple and clearly defined laws. It doesn't need to complicate things because it has no desire for more when it has enough. Nature only seeks to impart its wisdom onto man who, in his arrogance, will sometimes seek to bend nature to his own will rather than moving in harmony with it. Man's restless spirit can grow impatient and discontent with the simplicity of his nature and cause him to yield to the will of the stygian beast that pulls against the reigns of the chariot in eternal defiance.

　　The empire rebukes the simple laws of nature out of this restless arrogance. Time and time again, we have seen the campaigns redefine the square peg of manhood and masculinity to fit the empire's round hole and an endless barrage of not-so-subtle suggestions that we as men should devolve and become less than what nature has made us. That nature's design is somehow flawed and that the weak and happy slaves of the empire can do a better job than millions of years of evolution.

Trying to change the nature of man is no different than trying to stop a waterfall. Sure, you can build a dam, but the water and all its fury are still present. Without a way to harness that power and use it for something productive, that energy is just going to build up more and more until the dam breaks, and we have seen this time and time again. Nature's batting average is far better than that of the empire, yet they still like to play god and try to bend nature as they see fit.

A man who understands that his nature cannot be ignored and is capable of abiding by its universal laws will find the grandness of the empire and its globalist view unpalatable. His world grows smaller and smaller the more he accepts who and what he is at his core. The bread and circuses provided by the empire as a means to placate man's true nature are seen for what they are and offer nothing but indigestion.

He can only live vicariously through others so much before he again finds himself restless and searching for a more substantial fix. His nature is like a drug that he just can't kick no matter how hard he tries. He needs the blissful high that comes with embracing his thumos, and no placebo can keep him distracted for very long.

Just look at how many men today are living discontented lives. They've fallen into the trap of the empire's narrative that they are broken and must change to be of any value. You can see it in the eyes of every man who gave up a part of himself in exchange for a romantic relationship with a woman. He was taught his entire life that he must give up his own life when he gets married and becomes a father.

Men are abandoning their friends, brothers, hobbies, and interests because they have been brainwashed into believing that they have to if they want to live the ideal dream of getting laid once a week and, if they're lucky, a semi-enthusiastic blowjob on their anniversary. There's even the sad irony that when a man does all of these things because, *happy wife, happy life*, he is even complicit in denying his woman's nature.

The empire has made a ruling against nature that in order to make a woman happy with you, you have to give up all of the things that make her want you in the first place. Men and women are both simple creatures driven by their own nature, no matter how much they try to resist. The act of denying that nature simply because the empire says so is destroying them both.

Men that are good at being men are those that are most sought after by the fairer sex. Women are drawn to men who can help them survive and capable of giving them strong and healthy children that they can nurture and provide comfort. Men and women are nothing more than animals with the ability to reason. It should not be considered taboo to accept and embrace our nature.

Man's governance of himself is what has driven humanity from the very beginning. By becoming the sole proprietor of himself, he sheds the standards and moral code of the empire and its court of public opinion. He longer seeks the approval of those outside of his chosen tribe. As Roosevelt described it, the mire of mediocrity turns his stomach sour, and he can no longer pretend that he is content to remain among the masses. The need for external validation is now extinguished; he can now join the hunt within the wilderness of himself.

Life itself becomes beautiful when these simple truths are accepted. When our nature's simplistic laws are followed, the random distractions and arbitrary guidelines of the empire become easy to ignore. They no longer count. But it is getting to this point that seems to be most difficult for men who have spent their entire lives living under the rule of the empire. It's a challenge to realize that the laws of the empire can and should be ignored if they go against the nature of man.

His true nature is the sum of all of a man's greatness. He who can see the foolishness of the attempts made to quell who he truly is and the things that have become markers of superficial identity is free. He can look down on those who scramble along the ground, clawing at the meaningless nothings trying to fill their bellies with just enough entertainment to satisfy their urges for a little while longer is a man that stands above the rabble.

Much like those few days, I spent in the Appalachian backcountry, simplicity isn't something that comes easy. The constant need to complicate things and come up with elaborate solutions to our simple first-world problems is an albatross that hangs from our necks, preventing us from finding the straightest line to the truth. That truth isn't subjective to the individual. There is no, *your truth.*

There is only one truth, and that truth is, as Teddy Roosevelt said, *"We need the iron qualities that go with true manhood. We need the positive virtues of resolution, of courage, of indomitable will, of power to do without shrinking the rough work that must always be done."*

Any other "virtue" claimed by postmodernists to be essential is nothing more than the rules and moral codes that the empire has decided on. Courage, Strength, Tribalism, Loyalty, Honor, Integrity, Determination, Discipline, and Simplicity are basic fundamentals of man. You can add on anything you like, but by removing just one of them, you undermine the structure of nature itself.

Without these basic tenets, the empire is nothing more than a house of cards waiting for the slightest nudge to cause it to collapse in on itself because it was, in fact, built upon these very principles. Only when people began to add their own interpretations and exceptions did the basics get pushed to the back burner and left to boil over unattended.

The empire was a fantastic idea on the surface. Think about it. The idea of being able to forge bonds between multiple tribes and unite them all under one single banner is an exciting one. In more primitive times, keeping your tribe growing was paramount to survival. The larger the tribe, the more warriors, producers, and scavengers of resources you had. It made your whole tribe stronger. That is until it didn't.

No one stopped to realize that the tribe was getting *too* big. They were so caught up in the aspect of growth that they failed to see the downside. They made things far more complicated than they had to be as they brought in more and more tribes, thinking that bigger was always better. When one of the incoming tribes refused to assimilate to the ways of the empire, exceptions were made to maintain the rate of growth.

They never saw it coming that more and more tribes being invited to join the empire would cause too much diversity. They failed to exercise moderation, and like the greedy little fat kid in the chocolate factory, they got swept into the chocolate river and lodged in the pipes, and pressure started to build until we reached the point of no return.

It wasn't just that the tribe itself had gotten too big. With each additional culture bringing more and more diversity to the table, there were more and more compromises made in the name of being all-inclusive. Add to that the more recent boom in secularism within modern society. You end up with more and more rules added to the already convoluted and often contradictory list of expectations that citizens of the empire are required to meet. The empire wasn't a bad plan, but like any plan, it tends to fall apart the more moving parts it has.

Like the empire, a man cannot function if he has too many moving parts. Modern societal pressures and expectations topped with the constant battle for pluralistic status have pulled him in too many directions at once and left him immobile. True freedom is not found in having an endless supply of options at your grasp. It is found in having less. With too many options to choose from, you'll become paralyzed.

Analysis Paralysis occurs when faced with multiple choices. Picture yourself driving through the vast and empty plains that you can find in many of the fly-over states here in the U.S. when suddenly the road comes to a four-way stop. If there are no landmarks to indicate which direction you should take and turning back isn't an option, making a decision about which direction you should go is all but impossible.

You are likely to spend more time than you would like debating about which path is the best one. Reduce the choices to a simple left or right turn, and it gets a bit easier, but you will still be trapped by indecision. The only real freedom is when there are no choices. When the road is a straight line with no other options. You can only stop or continue going forward.

Simplicity and freedom in life are very much the same. Obviously, going backward isn't an option. Considered to be the father of existentialism, Danish philosopher Soren Kierkegaard said that *life can only be understood backwards; but it must be lived forwards.* Living forward is the best path but can only be taken if it is the only path available.

The culture of the empire is that of the consumer. More is always better, and people are manipulated into always thinking that they don't have enough. Sure, there is the modern minimalist movement where people opt to live more straightforward and less materialistic lives, but that isn't enough. A man can learn to be content with less material wealth, but what about with fewer choices? Think about it, there are over 1000 different brands of bottled water, and for some reason, people still think that one is better than the other.

It was the obsession with choices that led to the birth of all of these different brands. It's nothing more than water, but the empire has programmed people into believing that the more choices they have, the more freedom comes with it. It seems ironically appropriate that "choice" would be a weapon of the empire. Choice is oppressive in that it denies man the freedom to keep moving forward.

Simplicity comes with sovereignty. The sovereign man has but one choice, and that is to live forward. The sovereign man will live his life as he sees fit. He is not troubled by others' opinions or expectations, yet he works of his own volition to achieve status within his tribe. A tribe that he has chosen over a life of slavery within the empire with a true code of honor. This may seem contradictory on the surface, but in order to become sovereign, a man must shed himself of having too many options.

He cannot live a half-life and must be all the way in or all the way out. Remaining a citizen of the empire will lead a man to a life of forced service to those that go against his best interests and nature. He can choose this if he likes, but to do so feels like a violation of himself. To become sovereign and truly free, a man must determine that there is no other choice than to leave the empire. He must see that there is nothing more than existence in remaining in the same place and that Life, living is only made possible by his decision, the only decision, to move forward.

The sovereign man understands that failing to live forward will only lead to him being swept downstream with the current towards the jagged rocks of an unfulfilled life. He makes the decision to happen to Life rather than allow life to happen to him. The refusal to swim against the current will inevitably make someone or something other than himself the captain of his fate, and this is something that he cannot allow.

The path ahead will be filled with both glory and regret, but as Kierkegaard said, Life can only be lived forward. A man can always look back at the road he has traveled and all of the decisions that led him to where he is for understanding, but he cannot dwell there for too long. A man cannot afford to second guess himself and must continue moving forward using the wisdom he gained along the way.

There will be hard times and good times alike, and he must accept them both with gratitude and remember that had he made a different choice entirely, that path would be exactly the same.

CHAPTER TEN
KINGS AND HEROES

"That's the irony, the truly moral man is the one called most immoral. And the real scoundrel -who has no code who only gives a fuck about popularity and money and staying out of trouble, blending in with the herd, that man is held up as some paragon of virtue(...)"

- Roman McClay; Sanction I

Heroes and Kings are not born. Like men, they must be built out of a necessity. Kings need kingdoms to rule, and heroes need villains to do battle with. One thing that modern entertainment gets wrong is the idea that a hero will arise just when things look bleakest and will somehow, against all odds, defeat evil for the good of all mankind. It plays into our need to imagine ourselves as more extraordinary beings who would rise to the challenge and fight back the evil horde that seeks to destroy us and those we care about.

History, however, is written by whoever wins, so you'll have to take it with a grain of salt when you're told who the real heroes and villains were. I can't imagine that a villain who stamped a hero into dust would paint himself in a less than favorable light if he was the one who had influence over what would be written about him. Even less likely if he wrote it himself.

It's a question of perspective. Those who write the story are the ones who get to determine who the heroes are. Just imagine the world today if Adolph Hitler had been victorious. What would history say then? Even today, we are living in an age where the empire seeks to control the account that will be told tomorrow. It has already determined who the heroes and villains are, and anyone who stands against the empire and the code that it enforces isn't going to be written in a favorable light.

This narrative warfare that we find ourselves in is, in fact, history being written and rewritten in real-time. The leaders of the empire see themselves as the heroes of the story, and those that subscribe to the controlled media narrative, the sheep, being led to slaughter, are happy to follow along. Not out of any real conviction, but out of an aversion to conflict with the empire and the fear of ending up on the wrong pages of history. They have placed their chips on who they think will be the winner of this war and have doubled down.

Any man who possesses true virtue is seen as anti-pragmatic and a fool. The sheer notion that the tribe could withstand the empire's influence bewilders those who have already hedged their bets. The most popular argument for increased gun control in the U.S. is that an armed citizen doesn't stand a chance against the full power of the empire that holds the biggest guns on the planet. If that's the case, why should citizens be allowed to have any firearms at all?

Where this argument fails is ironically in its pragmatism. There are no heroes that had gone to battle when the odds were in their favor. Every tale and story of heroism is always laden with overwhelming odds that were stacked against the hero. It isn't heroic at all if the hero is the one with the most power. There's nothing heroic about a 200lb man fighting off an 8 year old who demanded his lunch money.

No, I imagine that many of the true heroes throughout history have been long forgotten. Not because they were humble, but because they lost and there was no one left to tell their side of the story. But today, such things aren't possible. This is the new age of unlimited information that can never be entirely erased as there will always be someone left to tell the story the way they saw it, regardless of whether it is ever widely accepted as canon.

The age of the empire has proven this. Just look at the mainstream media and the way they spin stories that are widely accepted by the masses who long for nothing more than to keep their heads buried in the sand. Anyone who tells the story from a different perspective is branded a conspiracy theorist and mocked by the herd. Still, we have seen a boom of independent journalism by individuals who only want to tell the truth to anyone willing to listen.

The empire has grown so great in power and influence that even when damning evidence against them is brought to the light, its citizens now simply choose to ignore it and turn their heads away. Not because they don't believe it, but because they don't *want* to believe it. The men who stand against the empire and cast light on the truth have almost no chance of winning, yet they do it anyway because winning isn't the only reason to fight.

It's because heroes aren't pragmatic. Codes of honor and pragmatism are like oil and water. They cannot ever coexist. For the hero, it isn't so much about winning as it is the fight itself. Heroes that rise against overwhelming odds know that they are almost sure to lose and that if they were to, by some chance, succeed, it would be by chance or luck. But they still walk into the fight because they know that someone has to. They are not wired to just lie down and be ruled and lorded over by those that wish them dead. They fight because they can't stomach the thought of not fighting.

The heroic man, the king, is a thumotic man. He realizes that it is not enough to just recognize that a villain exists, but he is drawn to that villain by a force that he cannot fully comprehend. He is compelled by everything within him to do battle against the empire that threatens all he holds dear.

This is the age in which we have found ourselves. An era where history is being written at this very moment and where the villains are no longer hiding and plotting in some secret lair but flaunting their plans to the world like a Bond villain who runs his evil plan by 007 before he tells him he's going to kill him.

Yet the people of the empire kneel and idolize these villains, these pragmatic men who have decided that the greater good must be obtained no matter the collateral damage or cost to the citizen. It has long been said that good times create weak men, and we have been living in the good times for decades now, but we can already see the tide coming in. The age of abundance has removed the incentive for strength, but we can see that the hard times are coming, and it is for this reason that it is time for men to become strong, not only physically but also mentally and in spirit.

Rather than waiting for the hard times to provide the reasons for men to finally take action, it is better to be proactive and be ready before they arrive. When the hard times finally get here, there isn't going to be enough time for a training montage. We're going to need to already be strong if we hope to stand a chance.

The time for heroes and kings to rise isn't coming. It's already here. The villains have made themselves known and have touted their plans openly because they believe they are on the right side of history. Kings and heroes must rise now and become the men they were always destined to be. Throughout this book, I have mentioned on multiple occasions that life within the walls of the empire has robbed men of the opportunity to become great.

This is that opportunity.

Just as we look back on our heroes of the past with admiration and awe, we must become the heroes that the men of tomorrow will look back on with the same reverence. It isn't going to be easy, but nothing worthwhile ever is. There is always the possibility that we will lose, and that thought alone is enough to dissuade some men from even starting. For others, it's not the fear of losing that stops them but the fear of success. Because with success comes higher expectations.

Everyone is so caught up wondering what will happen to them if they lose that they have failed to plan for what will happen if they win. What will happen is that we will be divided even further than we ever have been. The return of the tribe means a balkanization of sorts, and that scares people because they've had, *united we stand, divided we fall,* pounded into their heads for as long as they can remember, and they are too blind to see that we are already falling.

They refuse to see that if we don't separate ourselves from those who do not share the same values, we are going to crash, and every one of us is going to lose.

We must become more divided than ever before. There is strength in unity but only to a certain point. Diversity of race, ethnicity, and even creed can be a strength to a tribe, but the diversity of morals and values will destroy it from within. We are witnessing it now as the media clutches at their pearls about how divided we have become when we aren't divided enough. We must widen the gap between them and ourselves.

We must define our group. Who is in, who is out, and who are the threats we need to watch for. We must set up a perimeter and close the borders to our tribes. We must ensure that those within the tribe pull their own weight and contribute. We must have a division of labor based on merit instead of affirmative action or inclusiveness. We must do all of the things that the empire has all but outlawed.

We must defend the perimeters and strike down every threat to its survival. The age of heroes is not an age of inclusivity. Kings do not welcome everyone within their borders. They despise evils and those who wish to make slaves of their people, which is what is to come if men do not take up the hero's mantle. They must do it while knowing that they will be attacked and discredited by the low-level males and corrupted masses driven by an almost religious fervor to preserve the feelings of the fattest, weakest, and most useless creatures living within the empire.

The people of the empire are willful slaves, and their chains are only being made shorter as those in power continue to move further towards totalitarianism. The slaves have abandoned the thought of revolt and are now demanding what little freedoms they have to be rescinded further.

Freedom of thought and expression are on the chopping block. The freedom to raise your children as you see fit is slowly being eroded away by those that seek to imbue them with corrupt morals being forced down their throats. In the eyes of the empire, you are meant to be managed, controlled, and dictated while never questioning the authority of those who place themselves above you. They demand that you applaud them as they lie to your face even though you know they're lying.

"We must come together." Yeah, that sounds good but what they truly mean is that you must fall in line with the rest of them. You must abandon your morals, your convictions, and the sovereignty over yourself. They demand mindless and malleable drones that can be manipulated and easily controlled. They despise you for being strong and independent, and free because that makes you a threat to their dictatorship.

I am reminded of a quote by Frederick Douglas: *"Power concedes nothing without a demand. It never did and it never will. Find out just what a people will submit to, and you have found out the exact amount of injustice and wrong which will be imposed upon them; and these will continue till they are resisted with either words or blows, or with both. The limits of tyrants are prescribed by the endurance of those whom they oppress. Men may not get all they pay for in this world; but they must pay for all they get."*

Power concedes nothing without a demand and *The limits of tyrants are prescribed by the endurance of those whom they oppress* are the two lines that stand out the most. The elites that have placed themselves above you will never concede power and return it to the people so long as no one will stand up and demand it. The age of abundance has indeed created soft men who pose little threat to those in power, and until kings and heroes make themselves known, the power that the empire possesses will never be limited.

If those powers are not limited, then there will be nothing to protect you from becoming a slave to those wielding power. Douglas said that men may not get all they pay for in this world; but they must pay for all they get, and he was right. Becoming a hero isn't going to get you the accolades that you think it will but choosing to stand rather than kneel will cost you.

There won't be a parade in your honor unless you win, and even then, it isn't likely. But you will have to pay for what you get. Should you choose to sit on your hands and let everything be stripped from you in the name of the so-called "greater good," your account is going to be charged and you will almost certainly be overdraft.

There will always be a balance that must be paid in full. I myself am not prepared to have who I am or what I think become a crime. As a father, I cannot, in good conscience, willingly allow this to happen to my children or grandchildren. The time for sitting on the sidelines and hoping to just be left alone has long passed. Whether you choose to walk the path of the hero and become your own master or resign yourself to a life of slavery while letting your true self be chipped away bit by bit until there is nothing left, you're going to pay for it.

Heroes have always been defined by their monsters, and to those inside the empire, you are the monster. History is being written at this very moment, and what it will say tomorrow is going to depend on the actions of those who are willing to risk everything. That is what makes a true hero. The willingness to place themselves inside the flames for the sake of their tribe is what makes a king worthy of the crown.

A tribe that will afford them true honor and esteem rather than the hollow courtesies of polite society that reduce their own heroes to martyrs, half-hearted tributes, and shallow graves is where heroes and kings call their home.

The empire calls for your obedience and death. It demands that you deny your nature and everything that makes you what you are and that you accept their ruling that you are nothing more than a broken toy that must be repaired for the sake of everyone. You can feel the white-hot fire of the seat of life that resides inside every man calling to you. You only need to answer.

Your soul calls for a tribe of brothers that will stand beside you in the shield wall and walk with you on a path to glory, whether it be in Valhalla or heaven or right here on this earth. The path that you choose will determine not only our own lives but the lives of those that will come after you.

Right here, at this moment, you have but one choice.

What's it going to be?

Acknowledgements

    This book is a product of not just myself but many other individuals in my life that have helped me to become the man I was meant to be. First and foremost, I thank my wife, Melissa and our children. Without their unending love and support, I don't think that I would have written this book. I thank my dear friends Zac, Adam, Joseph, and Kiel who challenge me each and every day to be a better man, husband, father, and writer through their own examples. There are in fact many more individuals to whom I can give credit for helping me with this book, but there are far too many to list here without writing another chapter entirely. That said, they know who they are and I would like to thank each and every one of them for all of their support.

About the Author

Jeff Putnam is a father of 9 children, owner and founder of Rugged Legacy Grooming Supply Co. Having spent most of his life working blue collar trade jobs and seeing first hand the dynamics between the social classes, the main focus of his writings have been about the nature of man and his internal workings.

As a practicing pagan, he views the modern world through an ancient and mythological lens that feels true in his heart as he seeks to help other men understand and embrace who they truly are. In addition to writing, he is also the host of The Rugged Legacy Podcast which is available on all major podcasting platforms and a 21 Convention speaker.

Printed in Great Britain
by Amazon